WRITING
A
PLAY

Books in the 'Writing' series

Other books for Writers

WRITING
A
PLAY

Second Edition

Steve Gooch

A & C Black · London

Second edition published 1995
First edition published 1988

A & C Black (Publishers) Limited
35 Bedford Row, London WC1R 4JH

ISBN 0-7136-4175-4

A CIP catalogue record for this book is available
from the British Library.

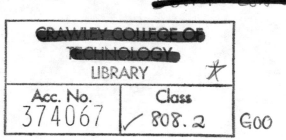
Typeset by Janet Watson
Printed in Great Britain
by Biddles Ltd, Guildford, Surrey.

Contents

for Christine

Acknowledgements

The publishers are grateful to the following for giving their permission to reproduce extracts.

Faber & Faber Ltd for text from *Waiting for Godot* by Samuel Beckett and *Betrayal* by Harold Pinter.

Introduction

Writing is neither a purely rational nor a purely intuitive process. Since the scope and variety of the intuitive side of that process are bound to differ enormously from individual to individual, it would be folly to generalise from one's own total experience of writing – feelings and all – and imagine that it could apply to everyone else. In this sense writing cannot be taught.

Any discussion of writing therefore, if it is to be of use to anyone else, must recognise the limitation that it remains in the rational sphere. At best it can offer a sort of climbing frame, within and around which the individual writer's imagination must find its own way. And yet intuition, feeling and imagination are the very source from which writing springs. It would perhaps be more accurate to say that having ideas can't be taught. What can be done is to offer suggestions on developing, shaping and actualising an idea once it's been had. Much of what follows then relates more to the time one spends *thinking* about writing than to time spent actually writing dialogue.

For many people with an inclination towards playwriting, the dialogue – once you feel sure of your material – is probably the easiest part. Dialogue tends to flow of its own accord – sometimes too easily – and represents the free, improvisational flow of the writer's imagination. It's the thinking time which is the most difficult to use productively. That time when the light bulb hasn't just lit above your head and when you're stuck, blocked, got yourself into a tangle, or when the blank page simply stares back at you defiantly.

This is the time, familiar to all writers, when the mind will much prefer to wander freely and engage with any number of alternative preoccupations rather than the job in hand. Whether it's problems of structure, a feeling that one's characters don't have sufficient 'life of their own' or a nagging doubt about whether the whole thing is 'dramatic' enough, nothing is more irksome than failing to concentrate, particularly if your time is limited.

If you find a way of channelling your thoughts towards the task in hand by reference to some sort of discipline outside yourself, this can be a great help in preparing the ground for the next burst of creative energy. Whether that discipline is supplied by practical knowledge of the workings of theatre, a writing group or class, a helpful friend, or even just a book about writing, it's perhaps better than struggling on your own in the dark. The ultimate lesson is experience: getting to know your own habits and processes and, above all, the favourite tricks your mind plays to skirt round difficulties or even, sometimes, avoid the obvious.

It would be a mistake to imagine that there is any particular time or place for these rational processes; that all planning, for example, should be done before one starts; or that while writing dialogue not a single conscious thought should enter one's head. Indeed, there are no 'shoulds' anywhere in all this.

Everything proceeds from the individual writer's original idea, and the best way to develop that idea depends enormously on the nature of the idea itself. What applies to an epic documentary won't necessarily apply to a two-character psychological drama or a ten-minute piece of agit-prop, and so on.

All this is to explain why I spend a lot of time at the beginning of this book talking about the importance of 'The Idea', and why what follows thereafter assumes a roughly chronological order from that starting-point. I'm not suggesting that this is the only way to do it – rather that, given an initial idea, this book offers a kind of maintenance checklist to refer to as you proceed.

A sounding board

The thoughts in this book have developed through some twenty-five years of work as a freelance dramatist, from working in half-a-dozen theatres as a 'literary manager' and, above all, from teaching. A number of students who have gone on to have their plays produced, win prizes and get commissioned to write plays have found them useful.

The ideas developed in a class I took over from a writer friend, Paul Thompson, with whom I collaborated on several plays a decade ago. When I took the class over, I was pleased to discover that my ideas about how to teach the subject coincided considerably with his. It turned out that Paul had based his approach on a method I'd proposed and which we developed jointly when writing together. During that process we had acted as a sounding-board for each other. So it can honestly be said that many of the approaches suggested here were discovered and tempered in the white heat of actual experience.

In any collaboration you are almost certain to have to articulate your approach at some point. And it is that 'sounding-board' function which so many writers desperately want. Some, it is true, welcome the chance to work their ideas through in isolation and prefer to show nothing of their work until it's finished. But many have a compulsive urge to show each page as it's written. And, since the opening up in the 1970s of opportunities for playwrights to work alongside theatre companies on commission, in workshops, through actors' improvisation and a variety of different playmaking methods, the need to open up and communicate the writing process has become more urgent. Whether you prefer to work with others or, working in isolation, need to be your own sounding-board, this book is offered fraternally to everyone needing to get the job done.

1
'What's it about?'

When people think of plays (in the plural), they tend to think of their fabric – characteristics of dialogue, setting, atmosphere, tone. The plays of Noel Coward, for example, are full of people in silk dressing gowns, with elaborate cigarette holders, speaking brittle repartee. The plays of Harold Pinter combine shadowy North London settings with a certain elliptical menace. Tennessee Williams writes plays set in the steamy South with sultry, yearning heroines barely disguising their deeper urges. Brecht means bare, open stages, simple narrative and songs. When we think about plays in the singular, however, our focus is different. 'Oh yes, the one about the tramp caught between the two brothers' or 'The one where that woman lugs a wagon through a war and loses her children'.

In other words, our appreciation of plays is torn between 'the world of' Noel Coward, Tennessee Williams or whoever, and the particular story-line. Immediately after we've seen a play, we may say 'I thought that bit where he strangles her because she left the top off the marmalade is a bit far-fetched' (even though it's happened in real life); but our longer-term response tends to remain with the silk dressing gowns and cigarette holders, or the sultry heroines with deeper urges. This can be misleading when it comes to considering the individual play. Of course atmosphere, tone and setting are important, but the question most directors, actors and audiences ask of a play is 'What's it about?'

This can be difficult to answer, especially if, for the author, the play's setting, plot and themes are all of a piece. Some writers refuse to answer, on the grounds that such a dissection somehow diminishes the play taken as a whole. Possibly there are circumstances when one is wiser not to reveal one's whole hand: in publicity interviews it may be better to stimulate interest rather than give the game away; with actors it may be better that they discover the reality of a part through doing it rather than talking about it. It may be that there are genuine ambiguities and nuances which are better left as just that. The 'life' of a play is often indivisible; once you begin picking at threads, the whole thing unravels. There is a very real sense in which to define a thing can kill it off.

On the other hand, it can help enormously if writers are conscious of what they're doing. Nothing is worse than spending several months on a play and then discovering half-way through that you don't like it any more. Or that it's turning out quite differently from what you'd initially imagined. A large number of plays end up broken-backed, in the sense that their second acts seem to be about something quite different from the first. The process of exposition, of digging in and opening up the concerns of a play, can be very different from that of denouement, discovering what it's about and tying up all its loose ends.

In one sense this always happens. My favourite anecdote about this is one I heard from Brian Clarke, author of *Whose Life is it anyway?* He said he starts every play thinking this is going to be 'The Big One', the masterpiece of 20th-century dramatic literature, the play to end all plays. Then, when he gets to the end, draws a line underneath it and looks back over it, he thinks 'Sod it, it's *me* again'.

There is no doubt that whatever one's aspirations, whatever the external goal one is aiming for, a writer's innermost thoughts and feelings are going to come through. To writers in other literary forms this may seem obvious. But, because dramatic writing is so much bound up with giving those thoughts and feelings a satisfactory external form (as I shall explain later), the danger of ambush by the unconscious or of losing sight of one's original idea is considerable.

Even a consummate craftsman like Arthur Miller can write 2000 pages to get 125, or work two years on a play and throw it out because it isn't 'the playwright's unique vision'. In this sense there is no 'formula' for writing plays. Each new play is a fresh challenge with its own special demands. As Miller puts it, 'You can create theater any way you want but it has nothing to do with a play'. Each 'idea' implies a structure peculiar to itself. And for that 'It's essential to be able to identify the main thrust of a work'. (Arthur Miller in 'Conversation With' Otis Guernsey, editor of the *U.S. Dramatists' Guild Quarterly*, Summer 1987.)

A 'sense of the world'

How can the central 'idea' of a play be defined? On the face of it, it can be anything: an existing story (from a newspaper or an old play perhaps); a simple visual image which sparks the imagination; a recurrent feeling one has about human relations or a social issue; a philosophical theme which seems to throw light on certain aspects of human conduct – any number of things.

ment one has that idea, whether the initial stimulus is
sensual or intellectual, all these faculties come into play.
ame time as you're thinking about how the play will
or whether you're finding the right style, your senses and
feel   are also actively guiding you through a series of choices.

It is these feelings which will act as motivator as you progress
through the work, whether consciously or subconsciously. For some
it's more productive to leave these feelings at a subconscious level;
for others, it's better to become acquainted with them as soon as
possible – to avoid their creeping up on you later. But, whichever
your approach, it's important to recognise the power of your
emotional involvement with it.

You may, for example, think you're writing a play about South
Africa, but in fact it's your sense of injustice towards your boss
which is really motivating you. As the play develops and scenes
unfold, you suddenly find yourself unexpectedly writing a powerful confrontation between a black mineworker and his white boss. It
may be something you hadn't planned. It may knock the structure
of the play completely askew. But it's the best bit of writing in the
script. Every other scene pales beside it. That's what you're really
writing about. That's your 'idea', your sense of the world.

It may be impossible to know this till you get there. Possibly it
may never even happen. So how can you test whether your idea is
worth all the effort of writing a whole play? After all, creative
people are supposed to have ideas all the time. What distinguishes
the idea that's worth pursuing from the one that remains forever on
the back burner? The only way to decide is to take time over it.

A play's idea is, after all, the most important thing in it, the thing
people are most likely to ask about it and remember it for. Above all,
it's your motivator. Whether the initial stimulus is external (a social
issue, a book or an article) or whether it's more personal (an image
which sticks in your mind or a feeling about something), there's
something you want to get off your chest. That feeling is your
reason for doing it, is most likely to propel you through the grind of
writing it and, if you temporarily lose sight of it, most likely to
haunt you later.

It's as well therefore to familiarise yourself with that sense, get to
know how it feels, remember its feeling and use it as a reference
point as the idea develops. Whether your focus is outward or
inward, your process more rational or intuitive, that sense you have
of the subject is the key to your relation to it, and your familiarity
with it is your best chance of expressing it successfully.

This is where the process of asking yourself questions begins, a
process which will continue until you finish writing. Is it an idea that

keeps coming back? Does it survive the harshest criticism y.
throw at it? If so, does it grow and take on new facets? Does it ret..
Its appeal – both to you and others you might discuss it with? Do
you begin to hear or see the characters, as it were, outside yourself?

It then becomes a question of finding the right story-line, the right
structure to express that idea dramatically, and the right elements of
plot and character to flesh that structure out. The longer you live
with an idea, the likelier you are to find a satisfactory dramatic form
for it. You begin to see it externally, as others might see it. This is the
first step to the play's having a life of its own, being able to stand in
its own right in the arena of theatre production. If you've lived with
an idea for some time, and it keeps getting stronger, there's a good
chance that it will end up *demanding* to be written – in which case
you won't have much choice in the matter.

Inspiration and perspiration

The element of compulsion is important. Far better to be propelled
to the desk (or the kitchen table) because of an urgent need to
write, than to drag yourself to it because you feel you ought to. One
of the dangers of being commissioned is that a sense of duty can
intervene between the natural development of an idea and its final
expression. Some writers even refuse commissions because their
sense of guilt at taking the money makes them seize up. Certainly a
commission deadline can hang over you like Damocles' sword,
reminding you that the happy combination of money and the
freedom to write are short-lived. On the other hand, it may provide
that extra nudge of discipline which many of us need to stick at it
rather than walk the dog, mow the lawn or rearrange our pencils
yet again.

Whether commissioned or not, for many professional writers
some sort of disciplined routine is a necessity. Knowing the time
when you're most likely to be productive and trying to clear away
any distractions during that time are part and parcel of living by a
precarious skill. Even if it turns out that you write less than the
target you set yourself during that time, the routine of setting aside
a certain part of the day and sticking to it can be useful.

Sometimes, by keeping your nose to the grindstone, ideas will
come which you might have lost, had you packed up and gone
away. By the same token, however, you may find that forcing an
idea produces less than your best work. Being your own boss can
take on an ironic ring when you find yourself standing over yourself with a whip. No one should imagine that the task of playing
both servant and master to one's own creative imagination

in two people's energy. Or, given the writers I
v with bad backs, stiff necks, migraines, clicking
poor digestions, that it's a job without its share of
ease'.

7

On a roll

The happy balance between discipline and the release of the imagination is elusive. But it needs to be sought actively. That initial, maybe idle, idea is your most important asset. It needs to be nurtured. Knowing how it *feels* is the surest guide you have to its consistent development. If structure is the spine of a play, then your feel for its idea is its nervous system, and the connecting thread between one part and another which keeps them all in touch. It is your main motivator, the reason you're writing, the engine which propels you and which, you hope, will compel your audience. If you don't get off on it, there's not much chance the audience will; but if you do, you've made a start. You're probably already writing.

This quality of a dynamic pressure behind the words is particularly important in dramatic writing, and in the live stage most of all. We've all heard stories of people mulling over an idea for years and then writing it in two days. Such moments are rare. But they do indicate the kind of head of steam which it's good to build up. For an essential ingredient of dramatic writing is that it *moves*, that it has its own dynamic, that actors and audience alike are swept along by the pace, rhythm and sheer vitality of the writing. The American expression 'on a roll' best conveys that sense of being swept along by a tide of one's own creation. It can be exhilarating and profoundly satisfying if you get it right.

Unfortunately it is equally likely to be totally deceptive. When you come down from your Olympian 'high' and examine what you've written in the cool light of day, you may discover it's all tosh. Nevertheless, that rush of blood to the head (or whatever it is) can serve writers well. There are some who can only write like that and rely on theatre directors or their own (quite separate) editing skills to make sense of what's come out. Others prefer to maintain a steadier progress, with passion and reason moving in parallel, keeping their original idea firmly fixed before them. Whichever way you look at it, understanding the relationship between inspiration and perspiration is crucial to getting to know one's craft.

Not the least of reasons for maintaining this balance is the curious facility plays have for turning out quite differently from what they set out to be. Much of the process of dialogue writing can be like an exploration in itself, in the course of which you can make unexpected discoveries about character particularly, but also twists of plot and quirks of speech. It's not unusual, in these circumstances, for these discoveries to take you into territory uncharted by your notes and plans, however careful. It's then that your hidden, secret motivator can sneak up and take over, so that you start writing not what you *think* you want to write, but what you're subconsciously burning to write.

There's nothing wrong with this in itself – indeed, it's arguably what you *should* be writing in the first place – but it can cause difficulty if you had no inkling of it in advance. Even in retrospect, it's better to ask what's really gnawing away behind this idea so that you can order the material and communicate your real concerns as lucidly as possible.

Transmission and reception

Some ideas, of course, are better than others. Steeped in enthusiasm for one's current obsession, it can be difficult to see your idea as others will see it. In this sense all creative ideas are somewhat arcane. By virtue of their originality they will present a challenge to their audience and initially, perhaps, be difficult to grasp.

However, theatre is very much a medium of the present tense, an immediate and social experience. It is a waste of its opportunities if a play is so obscure that the widest possible audience cannot appreciate it. Unlike a novel, you can't go back a few pages and reread. A careful balance has to be struck between the familiar and unfamiliar, between accessibility and innovation.

Recognising this balancing act is the first stage in the process of transmission and reception which writing for live theatre represents. What signals is this play putting out, and how will they be received? How will this look to others? Have I got the presentation of my idea such that an audience will see the same things in it as I do? With all these questions in mind, tentative consideration of the possible outlets for a play become meaningful right from the beginning.

Never mind the quality, feel the length

Getting to know your idea from the outside in this way, and asking yourself questions about it, is also a good way of anticipating any detours that may crop up later. And there's no harm in asking some very crude, basic questions.

First of all, how long is it? It can be difficult, especially for a first-time writer, to estimate how long a script will run when played out. An A4 page, single-spaced within speeches and stage directions but double-spaced between them, with inch-and-a-half margins, plays between a minute and a quarter to a minute and a half, depending on the length of the speeches.

Bags of space around a script makes it easier for everyone – especially actors speaking while moving and holding it – to read. On the other hand double or treble spacing can get expensive when you come to photocopy or send scripts by post. The layout opposite is one of many possible. Capital letters for characters' names, and possibly for stage directions, are sensible both so that they stand out and because they're quicker than underlining on a typewriter. I'm not sure of the grammatical correctness of a colon after characters' names, but with adequate space it isn't really necessary. (With a word-processor you may be able to put a character's name, a colon and underlining all on one key.)

The worst thing about length is not knowing whether your idea is really a 'short' play (a one-acter or lunchtime play of usually just under an hour) or whether it can properly be considered what the Germans call *abendfüllend* – 'evening-filling' being somehow a more satisfactory definition than that vague term 'full-length'.

The only thing to avoid is the play of between 75 and 85 minutes without an interval. This presents producers with an insoluble problem. Theatre-goers, even in the age of the television commercial break, are still reckoned to be able to sit for 70 minutes, but not much longer. On the other hand, even with an extended interval, a play of less than an hour and a half feels somehow unsatisfying. Not that this should finally condemn all plays of that length. All plays take their own 'natural' time, and there's nothing worse than one that's over-cut or padded out. But an awkward length will make it harder to get it performed. Somewhere between 75 and 85 minutes is a kind of Bermuda Triangle for plays, into which many have sunk without trace.

Placing it

The next question is what kind of theatre might it suit, and where is it likely to get produced? Unfortunately the two are not synonymous. Given that there are so few opportunities for the production of new plays, this strictly secondary consideration can become crucial. It's secondary because, if you're burning to write a particular play, you should do so anyway, and to hell with whether it's producible – let someone else worry about that – crucial because size of cast as well as set and costume requirements can tip the balance for or against a play's production prospects. Rarely is that balance tipped in favour of the larger-cast, multi-set, costume musical.

SHELLEY	Starin' out at the wheels. A face full of axle-grease.
GIL	I've med an offer on it.
SHELLEY	The box?
GIL	The whole thing! Max's Grandma died, so they're gettin' rid of it. It's a bargain.
SHELLEY	Don't you wanna do it proper, Gil? Decent job, decent home...
GIL	I tell you what. Do it tonight an' I'll let thee shack up wi' me.
MARSHY	(Comes over and dumps gear on him) 'EY!!

Scene Three   Outside the caravan, which is now Gil's. ALSOPP approaches and knocks. SHELLEY answers him. Autumn.

ALSOPP	Is he there?
SHELLEY	Who? Gil?
ALSOPP	Who else, the Aga Khan?
SHELLEY	It's just that Marshy's here as well.
ALSOPP	Oh is he. - Well tell 'em I've got their money.
GIL	(Popping his head out) Did I hear money?
MARSHY	(Popping his head out) Hello, Mr Alsopp!
ALSOPP	Marshy. Here's yours. (Gives him his wages.) By the way, I think Bernie wants a hand with the Whip. Dodgy wheel or something.
MARSHY	What d'you mean, dodgy?
ALSOPP	I don't understand machines. He'll tell you.
MARSHY	Oh. Right. (He stands there. Pause.)
SHELLEY	Would you like a cup of tea, Mr Alsopp?
ALSOPP	I think it was fairly urgent, Marshy.
MARSHY	Oh. Right. (Goes to go)
GIL	Hang on a minute. (To ALSOPP) He is off duty, you know.
ALSOPP	Not in the fair, he ain't. No such thing. Shelley knows that, don't you, love.
GIL	We're halfway through a hand!
SHELLEY	Gil! - Tea, Mr Alsopp?
ALSOPP	No thanks, Shelley. - Price you pay for a fun job, Gil. You wanna job where you knock off at five, go work in a factory.
GIL	It's past midnight!

Generally it is only the national companies like the Royal National Theatre, Royal Shakespeare Company and Royal Court which can contemplate larger-cast plays (requiring a dozen or more actors). Most regional repertory theatres can handle up to about ten, but they do proportionally fewer new plays. The majority of smaller theatres (including regional studio theatres) can't usually cope with much more than half a dozen, and in 1995 those small touring companies left are often looking for 2-handers.

I shan't pass comment here on the blight on playwriting these harsh statistics represent. Sufficient to say, their immediate consequence is that one has to think hard about whether certain characters are essential to the play. In this connection it's worth bearing in mind that, at present Equity (actors' trade union) rates, the cost of an actor for the average rehearsal and performance period of a play is about two thousand pounds. That thought alone is usually enough to get rid of all those unnecessary waiters, janitors, cleaning ladies and next-door neighbours 'just popping in' which clutter the dramatically unaerodynamic lines of so many scripts.

In case these comments are thought inimical to job creation (oh for theatre subsidy which would allow actors to work a proper apprenticeship and go on to pension age), it's also worth mentioning that not only Aristotle but many actors themselves would be likely to approve of slim-line casts. The first theorist of theatre with his notion of the 'unity of action' would hardly have approved of dozens of small parts and sub-plots. Similarly, there are few actors who enjoy (apart from the money) the task of turning up every night at the theatre to appear only briefly and speak only a few lines.

Another consideration when starting work on an idea is whether the theatrical style of a play is suited to the building in which it is to be performed. Admittedly this can be difficult to gauge if you haven't had a play performed. Clearly there is an enormous difference between a 1000-seater proscenium-arch theatre and a 50-seat room over a pub. Apart from anything else, the necessary acting styles are miles apart. And yet scant attention is paid, in my experience, to finding the right playing style for the right script in the right venue.

In this connection it's worth studying the differences in style between published plays intended originally for proscenium-arch production, and those written since television became widespread. Bear the differences in mind when you imagine the play in production. But since you're also likely to end up sending scripts to dozens of theatres, all with their own peculiarities, this point is perhaps best left at this stage as a reservation in the back of your mind.

Indeed all these considerations, though they'll become crucial at a later stage, shouldn't really *rule* your thinking as you start off. The main emphasis should be on developing the basic idea in a manner consistent with the thoughts and feelings you've come to associate with it.

But before we can go further, we have to consider the nature of live theatre as a medium. No use dreaming up a symphony until you know the instruments it will be played on. Not that it's necessary by any means to know all the ins and outs of the theatrical profession, its techniques and technicalities; rather one should be aware of the differences between this and other media, of the unique 'arena' into which one's words are being thrust.

2
Entering
the arena

Much mystery can be made of live theatre as a medium, and indeed a large part of its charm is due to the ambiguity and elusiveness of the simple act of mimicry itself. Is what we see played out before us real? The actors are, but their behaviour isn't. Although we know it's a fiction, there may well be moments when the pretence seems more real than life itself. Does this character *know* he's a phoney? Do we know more than the characters, or have they got something up their sleeves?

The relationship between the, as it were, innocent portrayal of a familiar reality and the more knowing game of consciousness between stage action and audience is capable of infinite variation. But the establishing of dramatic irony can be reduced to a simple, technical trick – you let the audience in on a single, not even conclusive, 'fact' which the character is unaware of. Acting, the simple pretence of being someone else, does the rest. Only the very worst of actors can ruin the spell.

Of course the 'magic' of theatre doesn't always boil down to simple trickery. The deeper the dramatist and actor dig into their reserves of sensitivity to human intercourse, the more resonant their make-believe. But a lot of false wisdom is propounded about the 'mystery' of theatre, usually based on experience of only a narrow band of theatre style, but eagerly seized on by amateur enthusiasts and hack reviewers alike, and elevated to the status of 'eternal truths'.

Over-impressed by these mysteries and eager to join the ranks of the magicians, it's all too easy for aspiring dramatists to swallow these 'truths' wholesale and thus limit their own artistic scope. From Jarry to Beckett, Artaud to Brecht, Grotowski to Julian Beck's Living Theatre, almost anything is possible on stage. As Miller observes, a play is more than just theatre, 'it requires a specific form' unique to itself, but the only rules about *theatre* a dramatist needs to be aware of are the intractable, practical realities of the medium.

Putting words into mouths

One of the criticisms levelled sometimes at dramatists is that of 'putting words into character's mouths' – an odd comment because, in reality, that is exactly what dramatists do. What people mean, of course, is that their sense of what the dramatist is saying with the play outweighs their sense of the play's or the characters' autonomous reality.

Whatever the merits or demerits of realism, the comment isn't fundamentally about realism or characterisation but about the persuasiveness of the illusion the playwright has put on the stage. The most passionate, subjective and tendentious speech can become acceptable if it is somehow 'justified'. This is another curious term – justified by whom or what? In a different kind of play the most arcane speech and abstract characters can be quite acceptable. Everything depends on 'the main thrust of the work' (Arthur Miller), the consistency of the 'world of the play'. Dramatists can, of course, fail to find the 'art that conceals the art' of putting words into characters' mouths but finally it is the vitality and conviction of the total world of the play which counts, more than notions of character or realism.

The dramatist's 'voice'

That art – the energy behind putting words into characters's mouths on stage – is a curious one. It implies a sense of performance, an almost exhibitionist quality, a certain lust for the relationship between actor and audience, almost as if there were a bit of the actor in the writer himself.

John Osborne's *The Entertainer* gives a clue to that relationship. It was written at a time when the emphasis of much drama was on a kind of social realism (and indeed Archie Rice's back-stage life is as important in that play as his life on stage) and the theme of someone's 'act', their public appearance, their engagement with their audience, is central to the play. It is as though Osborne were writing as much about his business and his own function as a writer within it as about a fading music-hall comedian.

In this connection it's interesting to note that, unlike the anonymity of television and film writers, stage playwrights are, however briefly, very much in the limelight. Reviews of new plays always concentrate on the play and the person of the author more than (as they would with a classic) the actors or the production. The sense of the author being personally on display is much more powerful than in any other medium. Playwrights are *expected* to have something striking and original to say, almost as if they were speaking to the audience directly, rather than couching their view of the world in plot, characters and dialogue. Indeed, audiences are much quicker to seek out and seize on the 'point' of a play than is generally acknowledged.

Dramatists themselves can often be reluctant to see themselves displayed this prominently in their work. They frequently prefer to think of themselves as back-room boys, sending coded messages anonymously, and often imagining that the representation of the real world they've created has an objectivity which obscures the identity of the author. Of course they would be only too happy to acknowledge authorship once the play is confirmed a success, but there can also be a genuine humility before the proof of the pudding – not to mention the anxiety that it might turn out to be indigestible. It is in the nature of the medium that a dramatist is both detached from and deeply involved in his work.

The origins of Greek drama in its development from the epic poem spoken by one person, through the notion of a two-person dialogue, to a maximum of three, give a further indication of the source of this energy. Whereas a novelist is describing, and a poet perhaps distilling, a dramatist is declaiming, not necessarily in the pompous sense (though that can happen), but in the sense of 'voicing' his concerns. Drama is far from being a private medium, far from that direct and one-to-one communication represented by a book, or even a radio play. It implies the consciousness of a live and present collective audience, and therefore a certain 'projection'.

Indeed the notion of a dramatist's 'voice' is closely connected to, possibly even formed by, this relationship between the playwright's own individual concerns and the particular public arena into which his words are thrown. On the one hand it implies the personal signature of the writer; on the other the form and style employed to get those personal preoccupations across. At its best it can refer to the individual stamp by which the playwright introduces and convinces us of the world of his play. At its worst it can become a kind of crude trademark: e.g. 'pinteresque', 'stoppardian'.

It can be fascinating to hear playwrights read, or perform in, their own work. A reading can reveal the closeness of the form to poetry – the rhythms and cadences of the dramatist's personal syntax can say much about the passion behind the lines. In a reading or performance we see the art that reveals, rather than conceals, the art. Playwrights invariably go for the 'meaning' of a part like no one else (just as theatre directors, when acting, invariably 'play' the production), leaving the trappings of their illusory reality as mere shreds. Nothing proves better the need for actors to heed the 'voice' of the playwright, and for playwrights to respect the autonomy of production. The very phrase 'getting it across' betrays the nature of communication involved. It also hints at the arena through which the dramatist is communicating.

Stage not page

That arena can vary enormously in its actual, physical form. Since the growth of fringe theatre, it can be anything from a room over a pub to the Olivier auditorium at the Royal National Theatre. With the massive influence of television on dramatic writing, the options for what is perhaps best called the 'pitch' of a play (how it pitches its 'voice' to reach its audience) are confusingly numerous.

Thanks to television, audiences and writers alike now have a heightened awareness of realistic detail in both speech and facial gesture, yet the theatre buildings to explore this awareness on any scale still don't exist. Too often one sees writing best suited to television being performed on a proscenium-arch stage. Occasionally one sees vivid, declamatory writing cramped into an intimate basement theatre.

Part of theatre's response to the age of television has been to create a variety of small, non-proscenium theatre spaces. The abolition of the proscenium arch implies a greater intimacy between actor and audience, a greater attention to detail, and less of the showman's podium. Yet in spite of the proliferation of smaller, experimental auditoria, there remains a terrible dearth of larger, non-proscenium-arch theatres where the techniques learnt in the smaller spaces can be given a wider application. The exciting development of in-the-round and thrust stages through the 1960s and 1970s – mainly outside London – has currently ceased. Meanwhile playwrights continue to cut their teeth in small, non-proscenium-arch settings without there being one major independent venue able to provide a focus for their further development away from the proscenium arch.

Whatever the actual physical shape of the performing space, its sheer function as the mediator of a dramatist's imagination is the paramount consideration. For playwrights it is best to think not in terms of writing on the page, but of writing on the stage. Because, unlike writing prose or poetry or for radio, you do not have a hot line to the individual reader or listener's imagination. What you write is not communicated directly to the audience one to one, but mediated through a director and actors, and also through the audience's experience of it as a collective body.

Obviously there are occasions when people do read plays on their own, but this is usually for study or as a preliminary to putting them on. It is quite a skill in itself to read a play and imagine how it might be in performance, and one that, surprisingly, is not as common amongst theatre directors as one might expect. Many are incapable of visualising a play until actors begin speaking and moving it on a rehearsal-room floor. It is what *happens* within the performing space that actors, directors and ultimately the audience engage with, not just the words.

A script in this sense is more like a musical score, meaningless to many people on the page, and only having life when it's performed. It is the success or failure of a script to animate a space and bodies outside itself which counts, not just its literal meaning.

The acid test

There is a philosophical, besides a practical, side to this. Playwright, actors and audience enter into a kind of conspiracy through the contribution they make to a theatrical performance. Together they conspire to put the deeds of the world aside for a couple of hours and recreate them in a pleasurable and enlightening way.

There is a hope that everyone will come away afterwards feeling in some sense confirmed. The playwright and actors confirmed in their various visions and skills, and empowered to employ them again. The audience confirmed in what they 'always believed', yet empowered to tackle new situations.

The balance between the familiar and unfamiliar, between accessibility and originality, is part of the expectations behind this conspiracy. Someone enticed by carefully edited critics' quotes to see a cheap, West End comedy (for which he or she pays through the nose) can feel as badly cheated as someone hoping for a lively evening who is confronted purely by obscurantism. It's a sad fact that the theatre, in a desperate and constant search for new followers, resembling that of the Church, sometimes resorts to advertising which would breach the Trades Description Act.

There's a kind of bargain involved here – inadequately represented, I might add, through the simple transaction of buying a ticket. The terms of this bargain, viewed at their crudest, are that in return for flattery and amusement, the audience allows itself to be challenged and extended, let in on the message in the bottle.

Judgement of whether the performance is successful is a minute-by-minute, immediate experience. Actors 'know' when an audience is responding, just as audiences get off on actors' pleasurable self-confidence. For every action, gesture, movement, line, there is a reaction – amongst the actors themselves as well as amongst the audience. A constant dialectic is established whereby the truth (*not* the reality) of what happens on stage is turned this way and that, viewed from one side and another, and held constantly under the microscope.

This truth is both played out and thought about, almost simultaneously. A play may urge the workers to unite, but the evidence of its action could be grounds for a breakaway trade union. A play may set up a character to shoot it down, but the audience may be more charmed by the character than the play. Each actor's 'reality' is challenged by the others'; the playwright's view of the world is checked against everyone's experience and belief; the audience's openness to new insights either rises to the occasion or remains boringly inert.

This is one transaction in which the customers aren't always right; they are playing an active, as well as reactive, part in the proceedings, whether they know it or not. 'The production was a success, but the audience was a failure' – how many times has this sentiment been expressed backstage? It represents not necessarily the arrogance of a failed performer (though it might), but the frustrated goodwill of the actor equivalent to that of the audience which was willing to suspend its disbelief but now wishes it hadn't.

This is the democracy of the arena. It can be manipulated, but only up to a point. It offers the challenge, to the playwright's 'voice' as much as to the actor's 'presence', of owning the stage for a couple of hours. And it's important for playwrights to remember this: that someone or something must be the centre of attention.

But any wilfulness of a playwright, actor or member of the audience wishing to grind an axe, and thereby playing less than the full potential of their part in the conspiracy, is soon found out by the other participants: the actor who, by drawing attention to himself, becomes an irritant to everyone else, interested mainly in the plot; the audience, looking for crude humour or sentiment, which misses the point; the playwright, failing to express his concerns through a convincing action. The only neutral party in the equation is the arena itself, lying there passive, inviting and invisible, yet full of hidden traps.

For me the great joy of theatre is its potential to display the widest possible range of personalities and beliefs in the flesh and see them, all equally exposed, subjected to the acid test of time. On stage real bodies move in real time. A performance sustained over a couple of hours is subjected to a physical rigour which occurs nowhere else. It has to have a connecting thread of truth for us to go with it. Far from being the instrument of state power or vested interest which film and television can become, and far from being the podium for self-advancement which many see it as, the arena retains its potential as the greatest leveller of them all. And not just because it can debunk, but because it can uplift.

It is after all relatively easy to portray an experience negatively – to set a character up in order to criticise it or send it up. But audiences, having made the effort to turn up, invariably hope to take some positive experience away with them. And they will find something positive, whether the dramatist wills it or not. What is transmitted is not always what is received. It's as well then, for the dramatist, to be able to turn the coin over and anticipate the audience's reaction before he pitches his material into the arena.

Time and tide

This is why I call it an 'arena'. That sense of a third force, outside writer, actor and audience, and yet being the site of a common experience, is vital to an understanding of the way dramatic writing functions. Your script will be moving bodies around, bodies with their own stage reality, within a space which has its own physical rules. It is the blueprint for creating a total flesh-and-blood reality in the present tense.

In this respect stage scripts are quite different from even film and television. What you see on a screen has already happened, it is frozen in time. On stage, however, there are no cuts and retakes. Every move, every gesture, every utterance is happening in the here and now. It is this which gives live theatre its enormous power, a vividness which is likely to stay in the memory longer than even wall-to-wall flickering images.

And just as the immediate present in real life is filled with a million tiny movements and sounds, stirrings, creaks and groans, body language, affinities and antagonisms, jealousies and indifference, solidarity and egocentricities, so the immediate present tense you create on stage has to be constantly on the move. For a live theatre audience time can never stand still. There is always something happening, even when no one is moving or speaking. Simply breathing can be a dramatic action filled with tension. It is important therefore for the playwright to place an action before the audience which, at the very least, is more interesting than the creaking of the boards beneath the actors' feet and the flickering of the lights above their heads. Time moves on, even when the play doesn't.

Actions speak louder

And dialogue alone is not enough. A character may, for example, come on stage and say 'I am an exceedingly honest, reliable and scrupulous person', but in stage terms this establishes nothing. It is, along with everything else that happens on stage, a mere gesture. Not until that character demonstrates its honesty and reliability through something it *does*, will its claim be believed. Indeed such an excessive claim is more likely to be met by an audience with mistrust. It almost cries out for another character to come on and say 'Actually he's a total liar'. For the audience the issue could be settled only when we see the two claims put to the test through what the two characters do. Actions, in this sense, speak a lot louder than words.

To think in terms of an 'action' then, of what *happens* on stage, is far more important to a playwright than the dialogue which, if nothing else is going on, can become 'mere words'. There are few things more tedious in a play than two characters simply conversing, particularly if it's a conversation about a subject the playwright wants to air but hasn't found a way of dramatising. Even what seems to be heated argument can boil down to the would-be dramatist's simply airing two sides of an issue through dialogue, rather than the argument being the culmination of some active conflict in the play which has reached a climax.

Because writing dialogue is a natural means of expression for playwrights, there is a tendency to 'write one's way out' of a problem. If only one can get the characters speaking, one feels one is making headway. This may work for the playwright's own benefit, or as a way of getting to know the characters, but it isn't theatre. And, however well tuned a playwright's voice is to the particular auditorium and audience he is working for, that dialogue may well end up as mere 'words in characters' mouths'. That's why the next logical step in developing your idea is to think through the 'action' of a play.

3
Bare bones

Aristotle's theory of the unity of action serves a purpose for would-be dramatists beyond keeping cast sizes within economic limits. It is also a useful reference point when considering how that basic 'sense of the world' which is your 'idea' can be developed into a play, not least because it concentrates the mind on what an 'action' actually is.

I don't wish to get into the pros and cons of Aristotelian theory in general, particularly where it quotes 'episodic' theatre as what *not* to do. We have in Shakespeare and in Brecht's 'epic' or 'narrative' theatre two examples set directly against Aristotle, both of which are perfectly successful in their own terms.

The point with each of these approaches is, however, that the plot, or story-line, or *action* of the play is the principal means by which its themes are expressed. Unlike a novel or a poem where description and evaluation can communicate themes directly, it is what *happens* in a play which is the principal vehicle for its themes. It is this conversion of the ideas behind a play into an external, physical conflict which defines it as drama and constitutes the backbone of its dramatic interest.

Where the action is

The idea of 'external, physical conflict' must immediately be qualified if it's not to be misleading. By 'external' I mean externalised, played out between the characters in the 'arena', and by 'physical' I mean that which is experienced through all the senses rather than just verbally or intellectually.

It's quite possible, for example, that the entire action or 'external physical conflict' of a play could be the story of one person's persuading another to change his mind. What happens here is the change of mind. All the means to bring it about could be verbal, and the change itself would take place inside the character. Nevertheless, for the audience (and indeed for the playwright) that change is external to them and a physical action in the sense that it is expressed through the independent 'life' of the characters on the stage, not just what they say.

In other words, ideas in the theatre find their ultimate expression in action 'out there' in that third space, the arena, the neutral ground between artists and audience. It is the persuasiveness of the autonomous, three-dimensional forces acting in that arena which counts, not so much the descriptive power of the playwright's or the characters' words.

I should emphasise here that, in talking about the life of the characters and their three-dimensional quality, I am not talking about realism (which I'll come to in a later chapter), but purely the fact that a dramatic idea ultimately finds its expression in the physical interaction of apparently independent bodies in real space and time.

It is vital then to find a central or main action for the play which will allow the playwright to express his themes directly through the interplay of these independent forces. It is almost like a chessboard on which the playwright places his pieces, complete with wills of their own, so that the game plays itself. And, as with all games, the question of what happens next is crucial.

The principal conflict

For this the choice of the principal conflict in the play is fundamental. Perhaps the test of whether an idea is inherently dramatic is to identify whether it actually possesses a central conflict and, if so, whether that conflict, in some shape or form, runs through the whole play.

It may be a repeating conflict which takes a slightly different form every time, or a continuing one which grows in dimension as time goes by. Whichever form it takes (and there are certainly others), it's more likely that at some point in its development the forces ranged against each other will peak and reach a crisis point.

Whatever the story, you are looking for a climax to the central bone of contention in the play, a moment where the clash of forces within it is at its keenest and somehow draws your idea and everything surrounding it together. Provided this is shown through something that *happens*, this can become the pivot for the whole play and, at best, crystallise the whole subject as it's been rattling round inside your head.

The main action

Once you've got that climax, the next step is to decide on the sequence of events which build to and lead away from that conflict – an overall shape which develops the potential of your central conflict to best advantage. This will inevitably vary a great deal from play to play. But just as your climax needs to be expressed through something that happens, so it is the events which lead up to and away from it which will determine the audience's principal interest in the play.

The theory is that all the events of this main action will somehow be as expressive of your idea, or main theme, as that central climax. In practice, of course, your story-line may well digress. Whichever the case, it's as well to decide, on the basis of your principal conflict, what the important events are, and to recognise them as your main action. This then becomes the spine of your play, from which everything else follows, and to which everything else returns.

Each action or event which contributes to it is then like an individual vertebra, knitting together and leading one to the other in a way which need not be logical or 'natural' but is at least comprehensible or has its own consistency. Aristotle talks about these events proceeding as a kind of cause and effect, a 'necessary and probable sequence'.

This is probably too rigorous a definition for modern tastes, but there is no doubt that what happens in a play and the connection between these events determine its themes (even if the playwright intends them to be something else). Just as striking middle C on a piano brings out the reverberation of all the other Cs on the keyboard, so your central climax will echo back and forward through the other events of the play, and vice versa.

The domino theory of play-writing

This emphasis on events and action is not to imply that a play has to be popping with incidents or fights, but that it maintains its own inner momentum. If the unique quality of live theatre is that it takes place in real space and time, then the sense of 'moving on' is vital. And it is through the succession of its events in time that an audience most directly experiences that sense of a living reflection of the world.

This doesn't mean that the action of a play can't be internal. It's quite possible for the events of a play to occur inside the characters. In this case it's the characters' changes of mind, the way their thoughts develop, the different way they feel about things, the way they influence or fail to influence each other, which count. In this case each of those changes of mind, each of those influences, constitutes an event which has an effect on others and institutes a kind of chain reaction. Whether between the characters or inside them, it's this chain of events and its movement through time which constitute the main action.

Central to a playwright's decision about the sequence of events in a play is, of course, the choice of where to begin and where to end. If you're happy with the focus on your principal conflict, there's a good chance that this choice will be self-evident. Where is the particular ball first set rolling which will end up being a time-bomb for the characters? Where are the seeds of mistrust first planted which will end in the characters' final alienation from each other? And what rounds these processes off? When can nothing more happen because there's nothing more to say?

By seeing the story as a chain of events, it often becomes easier to see which card collapses the whole pack. I'll deal with beginnings and endings in more detail later, but the main point at this stage is to find the core of the action, centred around a particular climax and chain of events, which is expressive of your initial feeling or 'sense' of the subject. Like cutting a richly filled cake, the exercise here can often be simply to know where to place the knife – measuring the portion so that all the best goodies are included.

What's your angle?

In considering a play's plot in this bald and schematic way, it's easy to forget that the emphasis of its story has to be as specific as possible, not necessarily in the sense of being realistically specific (though that may be important), so much as in showing where the slant on its events will lie.

If it's a play about injustice, for example, it will be important not only that an act of injustice is seen to take place, but that the audience recognises the injustice as such and not simply as, say, someone over-exercising their authority or being insensitive to the needs of others.

This is matter of focus. Whether it's on the fortunes of a particular character or on a group of characters, the treatment of characters' inner life, their personal concerns or private ambitions, will inevitably pull the audience towards involvement with them. It is an irony of many 20th-century plays that, in setting up a character or characters to be viewed critically, audiences have ended up identifying with them purely because they become familiar with them. Sometimes it is not so much a matter of giving the devil the best tunes as of giving him any air-time at all.

In other words, the extent to which one goes into the different characters' points of view can slant the action one way or another. An actor studying a part must, at some point in the process, find a point of sympathy with the character if it's to be understood 'from the inside out'. As in life, the more you get to know someone, however evil, the more understandable they become. Thus the more air-time a character is given, the more the action of a play will come to be seen from that character's point of view. By the time Shakespeare's finished with him, and in spite of his horrific deeds, even Richard III can appear more sinned against than sinning.

In this sense the arena becomes a different kind of leveller. Rather than undermining a playwright's or actor's attempt to abuse its privileges as a public podium, it can turn a playwright's intellectual intentions upside down. Within the arena all values are relative. It is the objective proof of the pudding which counts, not one's personal perception of it. Everything that happens 'out there' is subjected not to one's own private value system, but to the way human actions are perceived socially.

Let's return to our theme of injustice. I may feel personally that it's unjust to cut someone's hand off for stealing, but there are societies in the world where this is accepted. To cut someone's hand off for stealing a sheep when he hasn't is an injustice in anybody's language. It could even be a tragedy if you sympathise with the supposed thief. But if you identify with the authorities, you could make a case for it as an understandable, if regrettable, error.

The same story could even, given a cynical treatment, be farcical. In this sense scoring an ideological own goal is one of the commonest traps for a dramatist, and not just beginners. So not only is the specific choice of central action crucial, but also the circumstances in which it's set. One only has to compare Sophocles' *Antigone* with Anouilh's or Brecht's versions of the same story to see how the same events can receive a different slant.

Choice is all

In choosing a main action then, both the social setting and one's subjective involvement with the characters must be borne in mind. And not all stories lend themselves immediately to conversion into dramatic action. Sometimes one may have a story which, in narrative form (someone's life story, for example), seems to express a theme just as it is. When you come to think about it for the stage, however, without the benefit of that constant hot line to the central character's innermost thoughts or feelings, the story may come to seem much more straggly. Now that they have to stand on their own in the arena, certain important episodes and events may not fit into the main swoop of the action. It is then that one has to start making choices – something has to go.

This is often the most difficult time for a dramatist because individual episodes or anecdotes can be quite charming in themselves and seem somehow to epitomise the whole story. Adapting a book into dramatic form is typical of this dilemma. In a life story, for example, it may well turn out that it's best to show only the last two days before the subject died. Or there may be a particular 'high point' in a career which is somehow more typical than anything else that person did, and you can say most by concentrating the play around that event.

The point is that you have to choose. You have to choose where to start, where to end and what staging-posts to take in as you go along. But, above all, for a dramatic plot, you have to choose your central action, and once again the key questions are 'What is the principal conflict, and what actually *happens*?' It's often the case that the conflict one is interested in is internal to the characters, but it will be through the events of the play that that conflict is brought out. Hamlet's dilemma is articulated through his encounters with the Ghost, the Players and the others around him. Looking at the events of a story helps to crystallise in one's mind the decisive moments when characters are influenced, take decisions and make choices which then have consequences through the rest of the play. Once again it is this quality of the knock-on effect of people's actions which is the most useful in arriving at a dramatic plot.

Whatever the relevance of Aristotle to contemporary drama, the idea that a ball, once set rolling, follows an inevitable course retains its pertinence when considering dramatic structure. This is less a matter of rules than a utilitarian wisdom about an audience's capacity to take in the data presented to them – the momentum of events within a certain time span. Once you set up your characters and your situation, an audience's interest is bound to be led in a certain direction.

You ignore this direction at your peril. Everything you've set up will be assumed to have a consequence – sometimes of an importance which would surprise you. On stage nothing is accidental. Whether you indulge or frustrate the interest you've stimulated, the distance you can travel from it while still keeping your audience with you is bound very much by the delicate relation between the events of the play and the audience's ability to assimilate them.

All the world's a stage but the stage is one world only

Just as there's a good chance that the 'voice' of the playwright will be heard behind the words he puts into characters' mouths, so there is a sense in which that 'arena' where the events of the drama are played out is really the inside of the playwright's head. Fantasy can roam anywhere, and there are no laws about where a play should be set. Thanks to film and television particularly, our sense of dramas unfolding through decades and across continents has been greatly heightened. Why is it then – apart from lack of adventure and/or money – that the majority of plays for the live stage still end up taking place in one room?

One might imagine Aristotle leaping out of his grave at this point and shouting 'Unity of place!' But in fact he never said it, although many Greek plays observe it. The point here is practical. Unlike film and television, where a shift of place can instantly be registered by the objects and surroundings in front of the camera, what is on stage, live in front of an audience's eyes, remains the same unless it is physically changed.

A bare stage can be made to represent a living room and a clifftop in successive scenes through minimal props and dialogue. But there are dangers here. Because we have grown accustomed to film and television, there is a temptation to think that the live stage can achieve the same kind of realistic detail, and then change the actual physical setting before the audience's eyes as quickly and unproblematically as the arena in our heads. Apart from posing technical problems for designers and stage management – which, though real, should not in the first instance act as a brake on the playwright's imagination – there is a deeper aesthetic consideration. And that is to do with the associations in the audience's mind.

Setting notions

Just as action is more important than dialogue when it comes to an audience's ability to assimilate meaning through their sense of time, so their sense of space is also critical. Whatever the performance space, once the audience has got used to looking at it, it becomes associated with the characters and the actions that have appeared in it. To assume a sudden change of place on a physically identical stage is a leap which will take the audience a while to catch up with.

Even if the set is changed, along with all the stage furniture, and even if exactly the same characters carry on the action of the play, the changes that have occurred will need to be assimilated and, above all, their *meaning* has to be appreciated. Once again, nothing on stage can be assumed to be accidental. If an object or a prop is visible to the audience, it must be assumed to have a purpose. You cannot simply wish a piece of set, a piece of furniture or, come to that, a character away just because you, the dramatist, no longer need it. Even when actors forget their lines or a piece of set behaves peculiarly, one can rarely be sure that the effect wasn't intended.

The great advantage enjoyed by anyone working in theatre is that audiences are, in the first instance, curious and credulous. They want to know and are willing to be persuaded – or they wouldn't have come in the first place. But, if that curiosity is engaged by a set change in such a way that they spend the next ten minutes wondering where the hell they're supposed to be now, the object of taking them on through the story is lost.

The same thing can apply to the introduction of a new character (and is another reason for getting rid of all unnecessary waiters, janitors and cleaning ladies). Unless you specifically want to create tension by introducing a new, mysterious element, changes of this kind need to represent a sequential, rather than confusing, development.

Because everything on stage is assumed to have meaning, the central setting of a play gains in significance the longer it is on view. I use the word 'setting' because it applies to both time and place, and because it can refer to both a real place and a stage set. The latter can, of course, be quite abstract, but the stage designer's task will be to make that abstract setting contribute as much as possible to the meaning of the whole play and to obstruct it as little as possible.

In other words, the choice of setting will be crucial to the play whether, by being made carefully, it enhances its themes or, by being made casually, it works to their detriment. While there is no point in trying to do the designer's job, a playwright cannot ignore the significance of the play's overall setting, and where each scene within it is set. What's more, it's better to think about this before you start than half-way through when you've already become attached to certain locations yourself.

Frequently one discovers, in thinking about the span of a play's plot, and trying to choose where to set it, that the largest part of the action takes place in one particular location, but that a few scenes need to happen elsewhere. This is the messiest and most difficult situation to be in, especially if the main setting needs to be fairly realistic.

The problem here is that every physical detail added to enhance the main setting – plaster moulding on the walls, curtains at the windows, pot-plants on the tables – becomes a liability when you want to nip out to the phone-box round the corner, or down the road to the police station. The chances of containing a secondary scene within a single pool of light with total darkness all around are slim indeed. You could lay odds that the tassels on the carpet will pick up some of the light spill. Not only that, but that the audience – who up till now have probably not noticed the tassels – will be wondering throughout your short, but vital, scene, why it couldn't have been better lit.

The setting of your play then should not be thought of as an incidental background to the action but as an integral part of it. It's as important as the main characters and as likely to influence their actions as anything else in the play – even if it's only a matter of what they're likely to bump into. The setting has its own 'life' and its own significance. If you opt for a free-ranging story-line, going from place to place and leaping through time, it's as well to bear in mind that the designer's solution to the problem of what the audience sees from scene to scene will heavily influence how the play is viewed as a whole.

Naming the baby

Once you've decided on a setting and the span of your plot, the die for your play is pretty much cast. The principal features which will distinguish it from other plays have already, even at this stage, largely been decided. It's as well perhaps to stand back, take a more distanced look, and ask a few hard questions. Is it really as original as you thought? Are other people going to be as interested in it as you are? What is it about *your* treatment which makes it so distinctive? Have you thought through the principal conflict and succession of events comprising the main action thoroughly? And does the slant you take on them truly express your theme?

The first two questions imply yes or no answers and could be damning. Not only this, but the discipline of thinking your subject through, though necessary, can become wearing. A good way then of confirming or dismissing your worst fears is to become your own PR man. Imagine your play with a title, a sub-title and a publicity blurb.

This is, in fact, a serious and useful exercise, even if doing it can offer some relief from the rigour of thinking through. For titles you're looking for something that can stand as a banner over your work and both arouse in you the feeling you had about the subject before you started, as well as give an intimation of it to your audience.

A good way to arrive at a title is simply to play word-association games. Take a blank sheet of A4 and, starting with one or two key words, try them in different combinations and with different additions until you find something that sounds right. You may think of something better later, but a working title can be a great help in keeping your mind on your original subject.

A sub-title isn't usually for public consumption, but again it can help a great deal in focusing your mind on the nub of a play. Anything from an everyday saying like 'people in glasshouses' to a mini-synopsis ('the story of two women bent on the destruction of chain-stores') would do, as long as it sums up both the story and the point to *you*.

Definitely for public consumption (if only potentially), and perhaps the most relaxing of all, is writing a 150-word publicity blurb of the kind usually seen on handouts for plays. 'Locked in the grip of the sinister Mr Ardwell's plans, Roger and Cathleen know of only one way out. . . Will they succeed?' Apart from offering the opportunity to flatter your ego by saying nice things about the play ('this brilliant dissection of modern domestic life'), it can help you think through the plot and, above all, give you some idea of the tone of the play ('a wacky, zany comedy', 'a stark tragedy of our times', etc.). It should be pointed out that, given the brief timetable to which many commissioned plays are written and, by contrast, the extent of advance planning and publicity necessary these days, not a few blurbs for plays have in fact been written before the plays themselves.

Time and tide again

This premature exposure of your idea to the public gaze may well confirm your feeling that the idea has been done before. But there are those who will say that all stories reduce to half-a-dozen archetypes anyway. (I personally have a deep and idiosyncratic conviction that Pinter's *The Caretaker* is a reworking of *Oedipus at Colonus*.) And it may well be that it's in the treatment of your theme, its working through, that the real interest and originality of your idea lie.

To find out, you will probably need to do a little more thinking through. If there's a lot of plot, for example, it's important to try and think it through to the end. If you duck plot problems and hope they'll sort themselves out later, it can become very frustrating. There you are, 50 pages done, in sight of the end of the play, and your loose ends won't tie up.

Even if your play doesn't have a great deal of plot, the development of the characters can be vital. How do they change? What is their effect on others? How will they function within the world of the play as a whole? In this and other respects consistency is important.

If you've chosen a realistic mode, then the credibility of your characters' actions is paramount. Realism makes its own demands, the least of which is that what your characters do and say is feasible. But even if you throw realism overboard – in fact, *especially* if you throw realism overboard – there still needs to be a certain consistency to characters' actions, through which your audience can orientate itself in the special world of your play.

If it is a mark of identification, for example, that a particular character turns apoplectic at the mention of fish, this has to be firmly established before turning apoplectic at the mention of lamb chops can become at all significant as a development. Even if the point of a character is that it's inconsistent, you will need to make it consistently inconsistent if the audience is to go with your purpose. Saying that people behave differently towards different people in real life (which they often do) isn't good enough. There has to be a kernel of consistency towards which the differences relate.

Consistency in terms of realism can be overrated within the theatrical profession (as I'll explain in Chapter 6), but it is important for both actors and audience to see some sort of connecting thread to a character's actions, particularly if the other essential consideration – that of movement and change – is not to become confusing.

The passage of time affects us all – even if it only means we get older. There is therefore a sense in which the two hours of a play represent a condensed or speeded-up process of change within time. In life, of course, it's quite possible for people to be unaffected (sometimes stunningly so) by quite momentous events. In plays, however, there is almost an expectation that characters go through some process of change – certainly if it's not to become static or boring. Unless you want to make the point that they *don't* change, it's important to consider how individual characters relate to the basic situation, how they respond to each other's influence, what happens to them in the course of the play, and how they alter as a result.

A good way of keeping an eye on this process is simply to ask, every time a character is to enter or leave a scene, 'Where is this character coming from and where is it going?'; in other words, to spend a little time thinking about each character's background, what happens to them before and after each scene (or indeed the play as a whole), what their hopes and fears are, and where they imagine these will take them.

In essence, each moment in a play is like a slippery fish you can't hold still. It is the succession of such moments which constitutes 'stage reality', an elusive and fleeting thing, but palpable and powerful for all that. From now on our planning can only be a dry approximation, the bare bones, to what one hopes will be the life of the play when it is fleshed out. The value of synopsis and scenario, which follow, is not that they capture the play, but that they aid its writing.

4
Summing
it up

As the idea for a play develops, holding all of it in your mind can become more and more difficult. For Aristotle, it was the mark of a 'suitable subject' for a play that it could be encompassed by the memory or the 'mind's eye'. There is practical wisdom in this, particularly if you want your play to remain memorable for your audience. But modern plays tend inevitably to be either psychologically more complex, or more intricate in their plots, than Greek tragedy – sometimes both – so that some form of note-taking is necessary.

The very act of note-taking, however, carries with it both benefits and dangers. On the one hand, by writing things down, your choices become clearer. Instead of vaguely juggling a number of options in your head and not being able to decide between them, noting them down methodically can help you sort out the wood from the trees. On the other hand, the attempt to 'pin down' a play can rob it of spontaneity. It may be best to think of this process as a kind of 'thinking aloud' on paper, in which the hope is both to benefit from committing to definfite choices while not defining the play's essential energy out of existence.

Synopsis

It's at this stage that some form of synopsis starts to be useful. A simple summary of the play, half a page to a page long, it can serve not only as an aide-memoire for oneself, but also as a handy description of the play for other people. This can be particularly useful in collaborations, either with other writers or when working in concert with a group of actors.

Indeed, in any circumstances where more than one creative imagination is involved, the importance of putting one's thoughts down in black and white as an insurance against later misunderstanding should not be underestimated. It's easy to imagine you're all talking about the same thing before you start, but extremely difficult at a later stage to pin down exactly where or how you're differing.

A synopsis can also be useful if you're sending a script around to theatres. Given the dozens, sometimes hundreds, of scripts theatres receive, and the limited time and resources of the directors and others working in them, there's a good chance that only the first few pages of a submitted script will be read – unless a theatre has a literary manager or a panel of readers. The inclusion of a synopsis with a script gives people at least the opportunity to gain an impression of the whole play quickly and may speed its progress – either into production or apologetic return. In the film industry a 'treatment' (which is usually a synopsis with some sample pages of dialogue) is frequently used to raise money for a script. It's a useful way of selling an idea in both senses of the word – even if it's only to yourself.

Synopsis as de-coker

These are the conventional views of a synopsis – that it's either something written before you start on the play, or after you've finished. In fact, a synopsis can be a good way of maintaining for your own benefit a sort of running commentary on the progress of your idea at any stage of its development. Above all, the exercise of writing it can help clarify *at any time* aspects of the play which remain fuzzy, or which you're having difficulty with. Standing outside your work for a moment and describing it can help to ensure that the process of transmission and reception will run smoothly.

Most writers need to take some kind of notes as they go along – especially if, for example, they have an idea for the ending while they're writing the beginning. For some, the best notes are diagrams, perhaps with characters represented through initial letters, and even with arrows to mark their comings and goings or their influence on each other. A synopsis, at its simplest, is nothing more than an extension of this process, a way of 'airing' the process of trial and error which we all go through.

In this sense there is no such a thing as a 'correct' synopsis. Anything which aids the process of writing is valuable. And clearly the emphasis of your synopsis will proceed from your own principal engagement with the play's idea. For one writer the main purpose may be to think through the themes behind the play. For another it may be a question of working through the intricacies of the plot. For yet another the point may be to clarify the 'through-line' of the characters.

Whichever your purpose, the final effect should be to establish the broad scope of the play in your mind. Its main purpose is to give a simple impression of the world of the play. Even so, its ability to communicate clearly is essential – whether for yourself, when you read it back later, or for others. Within the overall impression therefore it's good to bear in mind the kind of hard information which will be necessary later – whether for yourself or others – to glean an accurate picture of the play.

For this the story, or main action, of the play, hinged around its principal conflict, is the first requirement. By giving an account of the plot, even if only up to a certain point, you orientate your reader within the whole scope of the play and remind yourself of the play's main emphasis.

A brief description of the setting (time and place) is also useful, and you can go into mood and atmosphere in a synopsis in a way which, as we shall see in the next section, is counter-productive in a scenario. Sometimes these latter qualities can also be conveyed through the sheer writing style of the synopsis which, at the same time, can give an indication of the style of the play.

The other essential ingredient is an account of the principal characters, by which I mean those around whom the main action revolves. There is little point, within a half-page description, in going into minor characters or sub-plot, nor in giving more than a line or two of tabloid-like description: 'Financier James Tempest, 42, director of Dowden Plastics, spoke to our reporter briefly at his Hampstead home before speeding off in his jet-black Porsche.' (I cannot recommend the tabloid-like style, but the balance of description and action is about right.)

You will need a more detailed sense of the characters for your own purposes, and you may indeed find it worthwhile to draw up potted 'case histories' of them, but your main focus at this stage remains on the main conflict within the play, and the manner in which it develops. If nothing else, we should be able to gather from your synopsis how the conflict in your initial situation builds to a climax.

Finally, a synopsis can also go into the thinking behind the play, briefly describing its themes in a way which a scenario – for reasons I'll explain shortly – strictly shouldn't do. The basic approach of a synopsis is descriptive, and its task is to cover the whole scope of the play, whereas a scenario is very much a first test of the ability of the play's events to stand on their own feet.

In the process of writing a synopsis thoughts can take on definition in a way which might not happen if they were simply left to rattle round in your head. It's an exercise by which you can force yourself to discover and define things about your story and its characters which up till now had remained vague. There is nothing worse in playwriting than fudging. Not making a decision about a character's exact motives, for example, can hold a play up for pages. Rather than remain as an intriguing ambiguity (as one might flatter oneself to think), it lingers as an all-encompassing fog into which the sharp outlines of the other characters and the specificness of their actions gradually disappear – along with the plot and the audience's interest.

As one progresses further and further with the play, the ability to make clear-cut choices will become more and more important. The exercise of committing oneself to a particular event, and particular motives, even at this stage, has at the very least the virtue of discovering what you *don't* want. Indeed, the benefit of all note-taking is ultimately as a kind of process of elimination. Eventually your characters will be making specific choices in specific situations, and it's as well to be as clear as possible about the options before you start.

There is no harm in constantly adjusting a synopsis – unless it be to become obsessed with it as a rather deadly end in itself. They can always be worked on further, expanding or contracting until you feel you've encapsulated the nub of your idea in a way which will be vivid to others and remain so for yourself. Neither is there any shame in modifying them later, even discarding them, if no longer helpful. But their function in airing your ideas, forcing you to think through their consequences and make choices, is invaluable.

Now this is the scenario. . .

A scenario has a similar function to a synopsis, both for one's own purposes and when working with other people. But whereas a synopsis gives a general impression of a play, a scenario is more detailed, like a working blueprint (see pages 38-9). As its name implies, it gives a scene-by-scene breakdown of everything that happens in the play.

This emphasis on what happens is significant. A scenario could, for example, be as short as one line per scene, and not much more than a page in length, describing only the central action and characters of each scene. But it's probably more useful if it contains all the relevant information pertaining to the scene and is anything up to about five pages long. It certainly should include any change in the time or place of the setting, every entrance and exit, each character's motivation, every action of significance, and any information reported by the characters which is important to the plot.

How this turns out in detail will vary greatly from play to play. A play set in one place where the action is continuous throughout a

MISTER FUN: SYNOPSIS

MISTER FUN tells the story of GIL and SHELLEY, a couple in their late teens, who meet in the spring while working in the funfair-GIL on the dodgems, SHELLEY on her parents' stall. After a brief romance, GIL persuades SHELLEY to live with him in his motor-caravan.

GIL is romantically committed to a life away from the humdrum, nine-to-five routine, even when, come Autumn, he is laid off by the fair's manager, MR ALLSOPP. His friend, MARSHY, though dim, is kept on because of his skill with machines.

With nothing to do, GIL's attitude towards SHELLEY's role in their relationship becomes more traditional - especially when it seems she is having a child. He remains fixated on the fair and, while SHELLEY is prepared to take odd jobs and study at night school, GIL drags her back to the fair the following spring.

The fair is now on a new, semi-permanent, municipal site. For GIL, part of the glamour has already gone but, even though ALSOPP can't give him his old job back, he agrees to work on commission, drumming up custom through a membership club.

However, one of the active members, DEE, is also active in a local community centre which is also interested in the site. While SHELLEY gets into video and politics at the centre, GIL learns clowning and befriends HUGH, Dee's husband.

The latter works for an electronics company and, in the summer, the two dream up computer simulated games for the fair. But by the following autumn Hugh's firm decides to take over the site completely as a 'leisure complex'. DEE has a breakdown and SHELLEY leaves GIL. The only way GIL can fulfil his dream now is as his pathetic, but commercial, 'Mister Fun' clown.

<u>MISTER FUN: SCENARIO</u>

<u>Scene One</u>:   Spring. A fairground. GIL and MARSHY are working the
dodgems, discussing the girls. Meanwhile SHELLEY and her friend,
WINA, are discussing GIL who's bright and thinks he's flash, and
MARSHY, who's very slow. WINA hopes GIL will come over and take their
fare, but SHELLEY (whose parents run a stall) warns her he's likely
to short-change her. It's MARSHY who comes over. And even when GIL
does eventually come over and flirt, we feel the banter is really for
SHELLEY's benefit.

<u>Scene Two</u>:   Summer. The fair. While MARSHY packs up their gear, GIL
is trying to get SHELLEY into his newly-acquired motor-caravan, but
SHELLEY wants to discuss their prospects together. All GIL knows is he
wants a life away from the routine. All SHELLEY knows is she wants
'something better'.

<u>Scene Three</u>:   Autumn. The fair. MR. ALSOPP, the fair manager, calls
at the caravan one night when GIL and MARSHY are playing cards. He
gives MARSHY his wages and gets rid of him in order to tell GIL he's
laid off. The fair is in financial difficulty. It's moving to a fixed
site shortly and, though he needs MARSHY's mechanical skills, he doesn't
need GIL to pull the girls on the dodgems. GIL protests - particularly
when ALSOPP implies he fiddles the fares - but the best he can wring
out of ALSOPP is a half-promise of work on the new site.

<u>Scene Four</u>:   Winter. A roadside. SHELLEY has found a menial job for
herself, but GIL doesn't want her to work - even though they're very
broke. When pressed, he reveals his fear that his sense of identity
will disintegrate if the responsibility of 'bread-winner' is taken from
him.

<u>Scene Five</u>:   Spring again. The fair. GIL has persuaded a reluctant
SHELLEY to return to the fair on its new, fixed site, on the off-chance
of work. The fair is now much depleted and drabber, and the best ALSOPP
can offer (besides asking them to move the caravan on) is a part-time
job for SHELLEY on the refreshment stall. GIL is disgusted when she jumps
at it, but she is astonished when he agrees to help organise a fund-raising
supporters club.

whole act will demand different emphases from one where a succession of short scenes moves its audience constantly through time and from place to place.

Apart from significant information reported by the characters – you may want to leave a 'trail' in an early scene whose significance we only realise later – what characters say to each other in their dialogue is less important than what they're *doing* with their dialogue. It is important in a scene, for example, that character A is trying to persuade or impress or intimidate character B. It means next to nothing however that A and B talk about leaving home. Any confrontation between characters needs to have some purpose. To leave a mere conversation marked in a scenario without indicating why it's happening, what has provoked it, or what the characters hope to get out of it, is to court the danger of an undramatic, and therefore boring, scene.

Unlike a synopsis, a scenario is better if mood, atmosphere and the ideas and themes behind the play are not included. You should no longer allow yourself to be descriptive, because a scenario is the equivalent of the finished play but without the dialogue. What happens on stage should now speak for itself – as finally it will have to – without the benefit of your interpretation. It is your first opportunity to look at the events of your whole play baldly, and decide whether they will stand up on their own. This could be a crucial test of whether your idea will work in the arena, for, like a model boat pushed out on a lake for the first time, you will eventually have to let go and see if it sails under its own power. A scenario gives you a unique preview of how the events of your play alone will speak to an audience.

When is a scene not a scene?

The definition of a scenario, of course, begs the question 'What is a scene?', particularly if the action of your play all takes place in one location and is continuous. Even if the play is broken down into scenes of only a few pages, it's useful for scenario purposes to think in terms of quite short segments of action – about a page or less. If we go back to the idea of the main action as the spine of your play, each mini-scene within that should be like one of its connecting vertebrae, containing its own miniature conflict and action relating to the main action, and leading on to the next.

A useful model for such mini-scenes is the way the texts of classical French, Italian or Spanish plays were laid out – even until the time of Jean Anouilh. In these plays a new scene is indicated every time a character enters or exits.

Entrances and exits

This is good to bear in mind as an exercise, not least because every entrance and exit should in any case be a significant event which distinctly moves the interest of the play on. Once a new character enters a scene, it should bring baggage with it. The playwright needs to know where it's come from and what it's hoping to get out of the situation. It should provoke a new interplay amongst the characters on stage, whether between themselves or in their reaction to previous events. It should definitely not be a sleight-of-hand by a lazy dramatist attempting to manipulate bodies into position when he needs them.

In this connection it is always vital to know why you've got a character on stage and what they're doing there. There is nothing worse than letting your dialogue between, say, two characters ramble on, forgetting that you've left a third character on stage, gooseberry-like, with nothing to do. Nor is it enough (certainly for the actor) to imagine that the character can read a newspaper, do her knitting or engage in other idle activities.

Every single body on stage, for the audience if no one else, makes a statement and is an active participant in the proceedings. Even if the statement is that the character is not interested in what the others are doing, one should be positively aware of the statement, not imagine that one can have characters, as it were, in neutral and bring them back into the action as and when one wants. Once again it's vital to think in terms of where characters have come from emotionally and where they're hoping to go.

In situations where your characters are on stage continuously, it may be necessary to think of other breaks or changes in the direction of the action to mark these mini-scenes or 'beats'. Any interruption, such as a phone ringing or an object falling, is one possibility. But more common are the peaks and troughs which occur almost naturally in any confrontation between characters. If two characters are having an argument which gets more and more heated and culminates in one of them throwing something, it's likely that this will be followed by a lull – at least until the next storm. It's here that there is a kind of natural break, a marker for the end of a mini-scene.

Similarly, every time a character employs a different tack (to persuade, cajole, comfort – whatever the motivation), this is likely to build to a certain pitch, then play itself out, before a new tack is embarked on. It is here that one can mark a beat worth detailing in a scenario, because it represents a new action. In terms of layout it can be helpful to mark each of these beats by starting them on a new line. Paragraphing generally is a good way to give shape to what can come to seem like a repetitious list of happenings. When you eventually come to flesh your scenes out with dialogue, it may be that a significant movement or gesture or pause will mark these beats.

Dialogue itself can be helpful to crystallise the essence of the particular conflict in a scene or of a character's particular manner of speech, but it should be used sparingly – only a line or two, unless, as can sometimes happen when working on a scenario, the scene suddenly becomes so vivid in one's mind that one ends up actually writing a draft of it.

Back and forth

This last possibility is not untypical of the relationship between all forms of planning and actual writing. If that relationship is working well, notes will stimulate actual writing and vice versa. Indeed, the best situation is perhaps where one is contantly stimulating the other, and where the writer can move freely between 'structural' thinking and actual writing as and when the Muse strikes. As with synopses, there is no need to think of a scenario as either incomplete or finished. If you've thought the plot through as far as you can go, that may be a good time to leave the scenario and start writing dialogue. Similarly, if you can get no further with actual writing, it could be that an hour spent on the scenario will be more productive than the despair of the blank page.

In the initial stages of writing, it may be that you can only envisage a line or two of what the characters do to each other scene by scene. As you come to each new scene, however, it may be that you have a more detailed idea of what happens next, so your scenario is constantly one scene ahead of your draft. After you've completed a draft, it may be that writing a scenario version of the play is the best way to tackle the process of editing and rewriting. By asking yourself the question 'What is actually going on here?', it could be that the wood finally distinguishes itself from the trees, and the worrying sense that you've overwritten, but are not quite sure where, comes clearly into focus.

The blueprint analogy is again relevant. By putting the structure down on paper, seeing where the bare bones lie and how they fit together, the overall shape begins to emerge. For those familiar with the way plays are produced, a scenario is rather like the first stumble-through of a play in rehearsal, when the actors have worked through the play just once and still need their scripts, but you put it all together to get an idea of the whole. The rhythm of the succession of scenes begins to emerge, as does the knock-on effect of one event upon another. For actors it is an opportunity to string together all the facets of their character in time and see its development. For directors and playwrights it is a chance to see how the overall shape of the play emerges. After all, the same event, differently positioned, can have quite a different meaning, depending on whether it happens before or after another event, and on who knows about it. And in playwriting there are few more maddening things than realising a particular scene or event should occur earlier or later, and then having to struggle with the consequences for each character of moving it back or forward. A scenario should help you avoid exactly this.

Above all, synopses and scenarios should be viewed as aids, both to the memory and as a means of 'tickling out' aspects of the play which are perhaps lurking just below one's conscious ability to actualise them. They are by no means compulsory but are strongly recommended as a way of breaking the task down into manageable chunks and overcoming the sense of defeat at the sheer, awesome momentity of completing a whole two-hour play. Like fire, as long as you remain their master rather than let them master you, they can make the difference between raw, half baked and well done.

5
Free
speech

The moment you start writing dialogue, the limitations of planning become obvious. If the scenario is the fullest expression of what you *want* to write, you soon discover, in writing the dialogue, the boundaries of what you actually *can* write. Inevitably a writer's scope for putting words into characters' mouths is limited by experience and ability. Very few people are Superwriter, able to turn *all* situations or groups of characters into a convincing and exciting dramatic whole. Just as painters rarely realise completely on canvas what is in their mind's eye, so the gap between critical aspiration and creative achievement is felt by no one more keenly than writers themselves. In Brian Clarke's words, 'It's you again'.

For many people, writing dialogue is like improvisation to an actor, except that you're inventing several characters instead of one, and on paper instead of a rehearsal floor. The source is largely spontaneous, and one line leads to another, 'feeds' the next like a stooge feeding a comedian. A more classical analogy would be that of the Socratic dialogue, where an argument is developed through question and answer.

However the method best defines itself for the individual writer, it is invariably a process of discovery, of articulating the conflict between the voices in your head. Yes, many playwrights do actually 'hear' their characters (though for some the visual sense is more dominant), and this is the first step towards dialogue. How it subsequently turns out can be surprising and can go either way – worse or better than you imagined.

On the box

The most powerful limitation on what we write is precedent. As Marx observed: 'The need felt for the object is induced by perception of the object'. How many times have people sat in a theatre and said 'I could write a better play than that'? And yet, when it comes down to it, we not only rely heavily on what we know from what we've seen and read, but we also rediscover for ourselves the difficulty of actually doing it.

The limits of what is possible on stage are inched forward only slowly by successive generations. Because it is a social art form, depending on the collective understanding of a number of people for its realisation (unlike painting or a book), theatre is one of the most conservative art forms. We only have to look at how the fortnightly-rep. values of the 1950s have resurfaced in the free-market theatre of the 1980s and 1990s after the experiments of the 1970s (some of which were themselves reruns of 1930s' innovations) to see how slow genuine progress is.

In this context it's perhaps wise to look at the influences on the way we think of dialogue and the way we write it. At any given point in theatre history the influence of the most prominent playwrights will be considerable. One has only to think of the Pinter imitators in the 1960s and the influence of the 'Howards and Davids' in the 1970s to appreciate the unusual individual power of stage dramatists in an age of mass media.

Nevertheless there can be little doubt that the most powerful contemporary influence of all on our concept of drama is television. It reaches the largest number of people and is the most easily absorbed. I say 'absorbed' because I suspect that the means by which television dialogue has influenced theatre writing are largely passive. It's easy to imagine that the words one hears put into characters' mouths on the flickering, small screen have the same function as those on stage. But there is a qualitative difference – not in the sense of good or bad, grander or finer, but simply in their function.

In the first instance television, like film, is photography. Whatever is captured by its lens is, willy-nilly, a real object. Much of television's product is not concerned with the make-believe of drama, but with the photography of real occurrences – sport, news, discussion, chat shows, etc. Throughout the whole range of its presentation therefore, the choice and placing of real objects in front of the camera are the primary skills involved. However creative and imaginative the vision of those behind the camera, both the techniques of the medium itself and the training of the viewer's responses will be heavily conditioned by this general function.

This is one reason why, generally, anything which departs from a basis in present-day realism – be it costume drama, 'expressionism', 'fantasy' – is more difficult to make work on television. As the medium becomes better and better understood, experiments in other forms of drama have become more and more successful – the work of Dennis Potter is a notable example – but the bulk of output from television drama conditions us heavily in what we understand as 'good dialogue'. It should be pointed out that even in Potter's work – however fantastic the situation, however clever the juxtaposition of present and past realities – the words that emanate from his characters' mouths are very much consistent with what one would expect a real body in real time to utter.

This may seem self-evident, almost a definition of good dialogue. But in considering what is good dialogue for live theatre, one has to bear in mind first of all exactly what an audience is watching. It is not a moving photograph of people representing life at some point in the past, but people in the flesh creating a representation of life in the here and now. The difference is crucial. Whereas on stage a make-beleive prop is acceptable, even perhaps desirable, in television it would simply look phoney. On stage actors actively create a live make-believe world; what we see on television are real but passive objects, photographed in the past by a camera behind which most of the actively imaginative work has already been done.

Dialogue as an old coat

The point here is that television dialogue, far from being an active ingredient in the creation of that make-believe, a live gesture, is part of the passive appurtenances of the characters, like their costumes or props. Although it needs to appear as real as they do, there is just as much artifice in this as there is in their 1930s trousers, run up by a theatrical costumier. All the artifice goes into making what appears before the camera to be photographed as convincing a frozen picture as possible. On stage the artifice goes into the creation of a self-activating illusion in the present tense. In this sense dialogue becomes something to be used, while itself active, in that process.

On stage a character can say 'Here I am in the Bastille in 1871' and, if there's nothing else but the walls of the theatre, we believe him for the time being. On television there can't be 'nothing else': we look behind him, see a no. 43 bus and know he's crackers. Much of the illusory world of a television play is supplied through what we see on the screen besides the actors. The set and other objects in front of the camera create a picture which passes on all the information we need about setting in time and place.

At the same time close-ups enable us to read characters' reactions easily without recourse to dialogue. The same close-ups – removing a character from a whole scene and, as it were, putting it under a microscope – make it more difficult for stylised language to seem convincing as it emerges from present-day lips on which you can see the saliva. In other words, the emphasis in television dialogue is very much on its seeming real, belonging to the characters and their surroundings, almost hanging on them like a coat. In live theatre, however, while this is important to an extent, it is what is *made* with the dialogue which counts, what it actively *does*.

The consequences of television influence on stage writing have been mainly disastrous – largely because the differences seem to be so slight and are therefore so easily overlooked. In general, stage writing has needed to become more 'naturalistic' (another exceedingly doubtful term) in order not to seem artificial. But at the same time writers have assumed the same kind of flexibility of time and place as is possible in television. They are simultaneously pinning down their plays in a realistic context, while assuming the ability to soar through time and space.

The consequence is a kind of stylistic disorientation for the audience. What does the action played out in front of our eyes really represent? It seems like a slice of life one moment, and then we're asked to imagine the same stage is representing something entirely different. In effect, the stage is trying in this instance to be a camera, a job it cannot do.

But not only writers have contributed to this confusion. The actors' craft has been equally affected by film and television so that scripts are no longer read from the point of view of the opportunities they offer for an active re-creation of the world, but for whether the characters, viewed as passive objects, seem real. This obviously begs a number of questions.

First of all, whether what seems real to one person's experience will coincide with someone else's; second, whether what makes sense in terms of the actor's craft on television will necessarily work for the stage in general, and for each individual new play in particular. Given the huge influence of television on the priorities and teaching of acting, it's important to ask whether what works best on television will necessarily serve new plays in the theatre.

Will the real Mr Hamlet stand up, please

I would gladly avoid all discussion of realism, since I am firmly convinced that it has become an almost meaningless term. My two principle grounds for this belief are that we should never forget that what we are creating is make-believe; and that one man's realism is invariably another man's fantasy – no two people use the term in the same way. Everyone responding to a play relates primarily to his own experience of life and at the same time is influenced by his own ideal of how theatre should be. Since everyone's experience is different – as is everyone's ideal – a discussion on this basis could end up with twice as many criteria of what is real as there are people present.

In considering these questions, it's worth thinking back to the idea of the arena for a second. Clearly an audience present at a theatrical performance is not expecting the actors to present them with real life – the closest the theatre came to this was with the 'happenings' of the early 1970s: an audience watching performers carry out real, if sometimes symbolic, actions with no pretence of a 'show' at all.

And yet there is a constant reference back to real life, and a kind of *frisson* the nearer you get to it. Again in the 1970s, full frontal nudity and simulated copulation on stage were the most extreme example of this. But the entrance on stage of a real police car or a real animal can still play on the same excitement. The fact of its being live entertainment, where an actor can fall or forget his lines, lends a permanent tension between illusion and reality.

By the same token, actual physical contact – striking a blow or pretending to stab someone – tends to destroy the illusion. Indeed, the difference between simulated and actual copulation on stage defined the limit not so much of what was permissible in terms of public acceptability, but what was aesthetically credible. In television, by careful selection of camera angle and subsequent editing, the illusion of real physical contact can be maintained. On stage, especially in non-proscenium-arch theatre, the 'reality' is all round.

This has consequences beyond the portrayal of mere sex and violence. The actual embodiment of imaginary actions on stage, especially given an audience whose sense of realism is greatly sharpened by television, demands that their actual physical re-enactment be as convincing as possible. While one may accept intellectually that it is the loss of the stage's distinctive theatricality which has contributed to its decline, successive attempts to emphasise its illusory powers – anti-naturalism, stylisation, neo-expressionism, etc. – have only reduced it further to a minority interest.

Indeed, the fact that most of our theatres have proscenium arches, necessitating in performance old-fashioned voice projection, automatically limits their potential to speak persuasively to a modern audience. While a coterie of theatre enthusiasts may accept, even welcome, the archaic conventions of old plays and play-acting, the automatic reference back to reality by audiences will render them nothing more than an amusing irrelevance to a broader public.

Against this, the kind of intimacy and precision possible in small, non-proscenium-arch theatres, combined with the excitement of live performance, offers an immediacy and power which – precisely *because* it has only occurred until now in small spaces – still has to fulfil its true potential.

This also has severe consequences for the use of language in theatre. For not only does it place a burden on plot and characterisation to be realistic, but also on dialogue to possess a kind of demotic accessibility. Indeed, for those who profess the desire for their theatre to reach a wider public, this must be a first requirement. Nevertheless it goes against the grain with those to whom live theatre represents a bastion of defence for fine writing against the incursions of the mass media. It may also contradict the power of illusion in theatre, that element of the unfamiliar without which the familiar is merely banal.

Stage reality

For it is not only the playing out of a dramatic action which is affected by this, but also the *version* or interpretation of reality it offers. Both are scrutinised fiercely by the post-television audience, so that the ideas of a play are measured sharply against their proof in the actual playing. Any attempt at a statement about society or an interpretation of the action is judged by the persuasiveness of the data offered. It is one thing to accept the satirical portrayal of a newspaper baron or a left-wing activist; it is quite another to be persuaded at the deepest level.

In this sense the democratising effect of the arena is powerfully enhanced. But whereas the 'reality' before a television camera can be selected and manipulated, the actual working out of an action on stage – with the degree of exposure it involves for both actor and playwright, and the degree of scrutiny by the audience – constitutes a considerable quality test of its veracity. Like a car rolling off the production line, the product has to stand up, to work of its own accord, to run under its own power.

There is a vital and unique autonomy to what happens in the arena which is found only in the performing arts. No one is expecting actual, real life to happen; at the same time everyone is keenly relating it back to the world they know. It is the persuasive power of illusion in this sense that constitutes stage reality, the truth behind a play which transcends the mere imitation of everyday life. It is this stage reality, the writer's own truth, which must be kept firmly in mind in all discussions of realism. The successful journey of that original 'sense of the world', which is one's initial stimulus, through structuring and planning to its eventual realisation on the page, depends enormously on one's understanding of, and feeling for, that autonomy.

What's more, in discussing stage reality it's important to distinguish between the contribution of the production and the script itself. The arena I've described above has its own laws as a physical entity, but these should never be confused with the traditional – and sometimes superficial – theatre conventions of the day.

What can be expressed in the arena depends not only on the skills and invention of directors, designers and technicians, but on the ingenuity of the text. A text which is carefully wrought can dig deeper, stir greater depths and extend the boundaries of theatrical expression further forward than any amount of mere scenery and light effects. Experimental theatre companies who rail against naturalism are quite capable of putting shows on the stage where movement, costume and other visual effects are stylised and innovatory in the extreme, but where the dialogue is more banal than anything on the most mundane of 'soaps'.

These are matters of form and style – important in themselves, but secondary to the playwright in the first instance. It is the specific demands of text, pushing the boundaries of *content* forward, which ultimately push forward the means of expression in theatrical terms. This consideration is particularly important for playwrights, whether in resisting the strait-jacketing effect on their vision of received notions of realism, or simply in combating spurious notions of what is real in abstract discussion of 'good theatre'.

Playwriting students often say to me 'I wanted to do the play this way, but (because they want to get it produced) I thought it would be technically difficult, require too many actors, be too expensive'. On the other hand, script editors and theatre directors (at least the creative ones) often say 'I love a challenge'. While these comments are frequently made (from both quarters) in connection with technical matters, they are rarely mentioned in connection with the more frequent occurrence of the billiant idea or plot which is blighted by slavish adherence to sub-Stanislawskian characterisation or tele-naturalistic dialogue.

The real challenge of theatre, often mentioned in abstract but rarely taken up in practice, lies not in a play's technical difficulties but in the unique 'fabric' of its text. Provided there is a dramatic consistency to the demands of the text on characterisation and dialogue, and not pure profligacy for the sake of it, playwrights should not be over-inhibited by technique or expense but trust their judgement and see their vision through.

One man's reality is another man's fiction

Many superficial comments are made about playwriting, some of which are mutually contradictory. Sometimes you will hear the criticism levelled at a play that 'all the characters sound the same'. The implication is that in real life people all speak differently, have their own syntactical quirks, and so on. Yet the same critic is also capable of saying of the same play that the playwright doesn't have a 'voice' of his own, implying this time that the data presented in the play is so varied you can't sort out what the playwright wants you to hear.

Both comments may be apposite, yet neither is particularly helpful. The implication that characters should sound as different as they do in real life is both dangerous and impossible. Not only is 'real speech' a nonsense – even in television there is much crafting of dialogue, of which removing 'ums' and 'ahs' and broken sentences is only the beginning – but everybody's personal syntax is as individual as a fingerprint. German academics have even programmed a computer to identify authors from a single paragraph of their writing. The expectation that playwrights could actually reproduce other people's personal syntax, even if it were desirable, is therefore a forlorn hope.

What, I suspect, is meant by the comment is that the playwright hasn't sufficiently identified and differentiated the energy behind each character's dialogue, so that one has the *sense* of varied speech patterns. This relates partly to characterisation, which I deal with in the next chapter, and is mainly a matter of identifying the different forces which the characters exert within the conflict of the play, and thus the different energies behind their speech and attitudes.

The attempt to have characters simply 'speak differently' can seriously disrupt a play's unity of style, and therefore the audience's orientation within its world. It would certainly unravel the playwright's voice. The probem here is actually one of style, of finding a mode which will successfuly orientate the audience within the world of the play – its values and emphases (the voice of the playwright) – while at the same time differentiating individual characters.

Write what you know?

A similar misunderstanding occurs when people say of, for example, a male playwright that he 'can't write women' (or of a white playwright that he can't write for black people). If we extended this principle to all writers in all situations, we would simply be denying the possibility that anyone can empathise with and write about anyone else's experience.

Certainly it will be more difficult to write convincingly about things outside one's own experience, but the whole of life is grist to the writer's mill. Even if there is much truth in the dictum 'Write what you know', the writer cannot be expected to reflect faithfully every single individual's personal experience nor to satisfy everyone's aesthetic ideals.

In the end the writer is thanked most for being faithful to his or her own truth. Everything depends finally on the slant you take, the artistic order you make from the disorder of life. The very act of representing life in art involves some form of interpretation, and this is the sense in which all writing is political.

Indeed, many comments about plays and playwriting, posing as artistic considerations, are in effect political responses to content rather than a genuine analysis of the craft. If the sum effect of a play is to challenge a dearly held, conventional view of life, the response will often be to challenge its realism.

Even within the craft a lot of misinformation about what is good and bad and, notably, what 'works' is attributable to the politics (with a small 'p') between the different skills involved. If an idea is unfamiliar and therefore difficult to act or direct or design, it's easy to say it won't work on the basis of previous experience. The point about new writing in the theatre *should be* that it hasn't been done before. This competition between skills can be particularly destructive in collaborative situations, or where a writer is working with a group of actors.

Whose 'would' are we in?

It is in these situations that the peculiar relationship between rational intention and imaginative resources comes into play. Easy enough to say what one likes, far more difficult to describe accurately what's in one's mind's eye. Few directors actually explain what they're doing (even if they're able to), and writers can also find it difficult to articulate their intentions other than through the script. In group play-making, everyone is simultaneously trying to be writer and director, as well as possibly performer. The need for a shared vocabulary in these situations is therefore paramount. A synopsis and scenario can help, but describing the fine distinction in style between, for example, vaudeville, music-hall and variety would test a Ken Tynan, never mind a group fresh out of drama school. Given the German academics' computer which makes a personal syntax as individual as a fingerprint, not to mention the differences between transmission and reception, the hope for true consensus is thin indeed.

Whereas a synopsis and scenario can be useful for a group of people working on a play to know where they stand with it, neither the more idiosyncratic aspects of their imaginations nor – unfortunately – their political desires are finally reducible to even the most practical schema. The nature of theatre work is so personal to everyone involved that the whole of their being – from their childhood to their political affiliation and what they had for breakfast – can be brought into play. This makes definitions of realism particularly hard to pin down on the rehearsal floor.

In this connection I should love to ban the word 'would' from rehearsals – as it appears in phrases like 'Oh, he wouldn't say that, surely' or 'But would he actually do it this way?' Writers don't generally commit a line or a gesture to paper unless it conforms to their sense of a consistent reality. But it can obviously clash with an actor's sense of reality. Both of these are subjective responses, yet they are frequently argued on the totally phoney grounds of whether they 'would' happen or not. Whose 'would' are we in?

Sometimes the issue is settled by a consensus between those present on what is real. Finally, every attempt to define realism in plays must come down to some sort of compromise or accommodation between what the individual defining it regards as real and what he regards as 'good theatre'. In most rehearsal situations actors are in the majority, in some they have the whip hand. So the issue is often decided on the basis of what actors think is real.

This is much more heavily conditioned by what will work on stage than by what writers, who usually take life as their point of departure, think is real. Admittedly this is only their observation of life, and usually from, as it were, the outside. But it is high time everybody in these discussions confessed that what they're actually talking about is a stage reality – usually an amalgam of theatrical experience based considerably on producing television drama and old plays, a large part of which can be irrelevant to new work.

In this sense 'would' means not reality, but what is generally acceptable to current theatrical taste. Many new plays present a challenge to currently accepted norms and can be undermined by this spurious invocation of 'realism'. In the theatre everything we do is a fiction. We *use* our sense of reality to persuade an audience of the broader truth the play addresses itself to. Just as a sculptor working in wood or marble has to go with the material he's using, so we employ our sense of reality as a means of making our interpretation accessible.

Inside and outside

Some of the difficulty over definitions in this area comes down to the fact that much of a writer's observation (of character particularly) is indeed from outside, while much of an actor's craft depends on getting inside a character.

A story which illustrates this (and incidentally also bears on the relation between scenario and dialogue) concerns a show I worked on which was worked up largely through improvisation. Every day the director and I would bring in a section of scenario which we'd put together the previous evening. This was described to the actors and offered as a basis for improvisation. The actors would play out the scenes, and in the evening I would work overtime, writing sections of script based on the improvisations but cutting and polishing the scenes into a viable dramatic shape. Every morning, when these scenes were presented in script form to the actors, the cry would go up: 'This isn't what we did yesterday.'

One day, fed up with this ingratitude, I brought a tape-recorder into rehearsal, and that evening, instead of spending hours on cutting and shaping, I simply transcribed the day's improvisations verbatim. When I took the resulting script in the following morning, the cry went up: 'This isn't what we did yesterday.' And it was true – though not in the way intended.

The process of improvisation is primarily one of *ex*pression. The fun of it is not knowing what comes next – just as the joy of writing dialogue is the discovery of new aspects of character, unexpected and felicitous turns of phrase, and so on.

However, the process of work on an actual script begins with an *im*pression, that of taking the script in and digesting it, before it can be expressed again. Once a scene has been read once, the fun of its first discovery can never be recaptured. It remains there for what it is and, if there is no other dramatic excitement about it, then there is no dramatic excitement about it, full stop. The same effect occurs when people try to repeat an improvised scene. Once you know where it's going, the interest is in *how*, and that means a lot more care in preparation.

In using improvisation as a means of play-making then, whether with actors or by oneself on the page, it's wise to bear in mind that, when it's first improvised, you're inside the characters and *ex*pressing them, whereas when it's read back, you're outside the characters and gaining an *im*pression of them. What is exciting first time round can seem banal, once you know the outcome; it's the qualities of tension and necessary progression which keep a play alive.

Although a playwright's observation is from outside, the process of writing dialogue, as already observed, can be very similar to an actor performing an improvisation. In this sense a playwright is writing from inside – getting inside characters' skins (as Trevor Griffiths describes it) in order to imagine how they behave in the particular situation. The same joy of discovery, of characters taking off in unexpected directions and the same tension of the unknown can be experienced while actually writing. But whether this written improvisation will bear repeating is no more certain than for an acted one. (It is somehow very apposite that the French for rehearsal is *répétition*.)

A degree of conscious shaping needs then to accompany the more inspirational flow. Knowing where events and characters are going, and have come from, gives a play if not a 'tragic inevitability' then at least that connectedness which enables an audience to relate it to recognisable experience.

This balance of outside observation and inside empathy varies a great deal from playwright to playwright and sometimes even within a single play. It is entirely possible for certain characters to be portrayed with sympathy and others to be viewed satirically or critically. This is not only an indication – sometimes even a definition – of the playwright's slant, it can sometimes lead to stylistic lopsidedness.

Nevertheless the suggestion, frequently advanced even by major reviewers, that *all* characters have to be equally weighted and three-dimensional is a false trail. Where the energy and stage reality of a play are successful, nobody gives a damn about realism.

For example, we usually accept plays in which the middle-class characters seem fully rounded, while working-class characters are sketchy (some Shaw, for example) because this is a familiar theatrical world, and we quickly see where the focus of the play lies. Indeed the effect here is largely subliminal. But there is nothing subliminal about a play in which the working class is viewed in sympathetic detail, while the middle class is sketched satirically. This is sufficiently unusual that suddenly, it seems, a statement is being made. This, of course, reflects more on the social limitation of both audiences and commentators within mainstream theatre than on the inherent craft in the plays.

Provided the overall focus of the playwright's vision is clear, bogus demands for realism are more likely to cloud than clarify the energy of a play's through-line. Popular playwrights like Stoppard, Bennett and Frayn all write within a kind of elegant, drawing-room comedic style, which is very English and offers genuine insights into more than just middle-class life. But is it real?

Generally speaking, the expectation is that what takes place in the arena has its own autonomous truth. Audiences expect, even positively desire, a playwright to do more than simply reproduce a banal and familiar reality. They want to hear his voice.

Even so there are genuine rules of consistency within a play and in its relation to the real world outside theatre which, once invoked by a more or less realistic style, are ignored at one's peril. Even a fantasy has to be consistent to its own internal reality. A character who has disliked cheese from the beginning of the play cannot heartily tuck into a chunk of camembert without distracting the audience – unless some new influence has brought about such a startling change.

Of course, people may be inconsistent in life, and aspiring playwrights often argue this. It is very common, for example, that people in life behave differently towards different people. But much of that richness of inconsistency which is so typical in life can be confusing on stage. Therefore it has to go. Art is supposed, after all, to order life. Internal consistency rates higher than a slavish adherence to would-be realism.

A life of their own

As you begin to write dialogue then, characters can go off not on 'their' own but where the consistency of your stage reality takes them. This bears on the relationship between scenario and dialogue, in that, for the play to convince or persuade even oneself, one may find oneself led into a more complicated reality than anticipated. A 20-minute sketch may end up as trilogy, an epic as a one-acter.

Whichever way it goes, you are almost certain to have to adjust the scenario. There are always nuances of character and behaviour, unearthed by the dialogue, which you could not foresee at scenario stage. It may also be that the demands of your own realism – or the consistency of your fantasy world – mean that you have to shift the emphasis of a scene. The sheer logistics of moving bodies around the stage, or working out who-knows-what-when, may mean that you have to change the sequence of events. The more your scenario is thought through and faithful to your original intention, the less likely this is, but there is no shame in changing it as you go along.

It's almost certain, for example, that discoveries you make about character and intricacies of plot, while writing the early part of a play, will have a knock-on effect towards the end. Whatever your work method, you would need to keep some kind of note of this. If you have already projected such an effect in your scenario, it's a lot easier to see the difference a change would make than if you're trying to keep it all in your head. Also, if a change raises serious objections to your original plans, it's a lot more difficult to kid yourself that they will somehow work themselves out.

The spectre of fudging is nowhere worse than in revision. Changes of nuance can be so slight that one may think them imperceptible or of no consequence. But they can be exactly the kind of false ambiguity (where the playwright has in fact considered two options and simply cannot make the choice) which will leave an audience stranded in the grey fog of incomprehension. It is better to give yourself a little work at this stage and choose between two options than to get into such an unresolvable tangle later that you can't finish a three-quarters-written play.

The extent to which dialogue is a natural means of expression varies considerably from writer to writer. Some are so at home with the spoken word that they never attempt poetry or prose writing. For others dialogue remains an illustrative effect, almost as it would be in a novel or screenplay treatment, coming after the establishment of physical action or visual image. Some playwrights are incapable of shaping dialogue – they simply write reams of it and rely on a director to cut, shape and plan. Since it's a rare situation to have a director standing by ready, willing – and above all able – to do that, it's perhaps better to consider how one can shape one's own material.

Speaking when spoken to

For many playwrights dialogue comes so easily, it's almost a menace. To imagine that the simple representation of people speaking to each other constitutes a play is false. Thinking in terms of characters speaking lines to each other can become such a habit that a whole script can appear in dialogue form and yet never be a play – simply because there is no real tension and nothing really happens.

Playwrights often use dialogue as a way of establishing character and situation for themselves, particularly in a realistic setting, but they can also use it as a way of building up data throughout the play as a whole. Much of this isn't necessary. All we're really doing by this is making notes to ourself on character, setting and plot in dialogue form. Useful though this may be in a first draft to 'get into' the characters and the play as a whole, it is, strictly speaking, a misuse of dialogue.

Speaking dialogue should, as it were, be the last thing a character does, not the first. And only because it's absolutely necessary. It should be almost as if the lines were forced out — from sheer necessity, that there is such an urgency in the *situation*, in the point of conflict between the characters, that speech is the only solution. Only when the *situation* is speaking urgently to them, do characters really need to reply.

To say is to do

Dialogue in this sense is like just another gesture and takes its place alongside all the other gestures characters can make to express themselves in their given situation. Nothing is more boring in plays than characters making endless cups of tea. But if, for example 'I'll make a cup of tea' actually means 'I've had enough of this argument, I want to leave the room', then it has value as a gesture.

In other words, if a play is not to descend to the level of mere conversation, there should always be a subtext, something going on inside or between the characters, of which the dialogue is a necessary expression. It's a good exercise, particularly when rewriting, to look at every line of dialogue and try to think of a gesture which could express the same sentiment. Imagine the play in mime, and try to see how each line would be expressed. Those lines which don't translate into a physical gesture may well be redundant because there's no need for them; nothing is actually happening behind them.

Writing dialogue can therefore work in a number of different ways. Sometimes it can open up the play, help you discover new territory; at other times it becomes the trees for which you can't see the wood. It's helpful to know when it's doing which.

The two processes – conscious planning and inspirational dialogue-writing – are so different in themselves and require such a different kind of concentration that they will almost certainly work in different directions. The inventive, creative part of one's mind can easily feel hamstrung by the scenario, while the conscious and critical side could well be totally bewildered by the way the dialogue comes out. Bringing them together – purpose and raw energy – lends a play the dynamic which distinguishes it from mere dialogue-writing.

It may not be possible to pursue them simultaneously, but there's no reason why one shouldn't try to alternate them. In this case it's perhaps better to reserve the different kinds of work for different sessions: on Monday write, on Tuesday plan, etc.; or write till you dry up, then take a step back and look at the whole thing; plan for a while, then when you're sick of thinking through, try some dialogue.

Certainly, as you start work on each session, it can be helpful to look back over your scenario and see what you intended. Even if you've already departed from your plan, or your head of steam has built up and you want to go with it while it lasts, a simple résumé of what happened last, and what you'd like to do with the next scene, can be enough to keep you on the right track.

To sum up then, the scenario shouldn't become a straitjacket, hampering your ability to create; rather, it should be seen as a means of avoiding the kind of confusion which stops you creating. It's very easy indeed to be taken down interesting byways by one's characters. These can become so interesting that one finds one has written two hours of material and still hasn't said what one set out to.

It may even turn out that what one has in fact written is more interesting than what one intended, in which case there is no dishonour in changing the scenario completely and perhaps writing a completely different play. What you started with could always form the basis for yet another play. At least one playwright of my acquaintance makes a living from this kind of recycling process. But, if you do go off on a new tack, you'll need a new scenario. On the other hand, if the new material is less interesting, your original scenario will still be a good reference point for choosing between what does fulfil your initial intention and what is fascinating but extraneous background material.

In this sense nothing one writes is wasted. Any of the false turnings one may have taken, notes on characters, drafts of discarded scenes, all of this – if it doesn't turn into another, separate play – will be contributing to the mental data bank behind the final version.

For this reason it's sensible not to throw anything away. You may be unhappy with a draft of a scene on Wednesday, but come Friday (after the dustman's been) you'll wish you could remember what it was you discovered in it about a particular character. Or maybe there was one line which summed it all up – though at the time it was in the wrong place. A good tip for this eventuality is to use a loose-leaf binder and simply keep all those discarded drafts and other bits and pieces at the back, so that what seems irrelevant today isn't lost when you rediscover its importance tomorrow.

There may come a time when your soul cries out to slough off all this accumulated data (including the scenario), and the gesture of consigning it all to flames is important. But you can always do what a friend of mine did with a book that was later published – go through the ritual of burning it, but leave a copy with a friend.

6
The forces
with you

If characters in plays are not real people but inhabitants of that separate world within the author's head, by what criterion can characterisation be judged effective? In seeking an answer it's interesting to look at the different ways in which characterisation has operated throughout the history of theatre.

In Greek theatre characters were near-gods; in medieval theatre they represented moral forces; in *commedia dell'arte* the masks and costumes of the characters suggested comic archetypes; in Shakespeare characters tend towards the stature of the heroic renaissance individual; in Restoration Comedy the characters often represent different social types – *The Country Wife*, the fop, the rake, etc.; in German Expressionism characters represent a general social class – 'the worker', 'the small investor', and so on. Within the past two decades fictional characters like Chandler's Philip Marlowe, or personae like Marilyn Monroe's screen personality, have even assumed independent life and been resurrected as modern myths.

You might deduce from this that characters can be anything – ghosts, angels, animals, robots, parts of the anatomy, pieces of food – and so they can. The idea that they should be real people is a relatively recent development. But in considering what they *need* to be, one has to look at their function.

Hidden forces

Most people agree that the essential ingredient in drama is conflict, and essential to conflict are sides. Whether they're gods or represent a particular human trait or foible, the dramatis personae of a play are involved in a struggle. It doesn't have to be a violent physical struggle, and it needn't involve people. It could be a carton of cream making up its mind to embrace a tin of peaches. But, however they're dressed up, what all characters do in all kinds of plays is act as a force. They represent a kind of momentum — be it towards good or evil, hesitancy or decisiveness, obstinacy or acquiescence, conflict or peace, truth or deception, and so on.

Any character in any play in the end boils down to a kind of energy field directed towards a particular quality. Whether it's Oedipus, Tartuffe, Hamlet, Hedda Gabler or Mother Courage, there's a will behind the character towards a desired goal – however passive and however complicated.

The idea of dramatic characters being simply forces is, of course, at odds with the commonly accepted contemporary view where all the emphasis is on their being well rounded, three-dimensional, convincing and so on. Aside from the tendency of film and television (remarked on in the previous chapter) to turn characters into passive objects, it's interesting to note that these expressions are used more widely than 'real' as terms of approval.

Similarly 'caricature', 'stereotype' and 'mere puppets' are used more as terms of disapproval of characterisation than simply 'unreal' or even 'unbelievable'. It's as if there is a subconscious acceptance of artifice, even when most contemporary opinion pulls towards 'real life', as though the historical function of character is at work subliminally, pulling people back from wholesale acceptance of 'realism' on stage, even though, intellectually, nothing is offered as an alternative.

One only has to teach playwriting or work as a literary manager in a theatre to appreciate the massive variety of possible approaches to characterisation in submitted scripts. This applies even within the narrow band of work which is trying to be realistic, let alone that which is trying to be more experimental. It's also interesting that the conventional battery of critical armoury brought to bear on would-be realism is dropped immediately when audiences (including reviewers) are confronted by experimental work.

Whether the emphasis is on the physical aspects of theatre – dance and movement – or the visual, whether the style is exaggerated or 'outfront' as in cabaret, suddenly all the arguments about characters being well rounded and convincing become irrelevant. People then fall back on appreciative comments about how good the technique of the artists is and how entertaining the work is as a whole. There is, in fact, no serious critical criterion by which to judge such work. Unable to fly in the face of the obvious (that it's all illusion), the myth of realism still hangs like a heavy cloud over our critical judgements.

Pulling strings

Where the popular view of characterisation does hit the nail on the head is in its dislike of 'mere puppets'. In my view it's not so much an insistence on realism that concerns audiences (though that's what it's often mistaken for and where such discussions inevitably lead) as a resistance to apparent manipulation. The author is usually writing about a reality we all share and can see and hear for ourselves. What he's writing about connects in some way with *our* lives (which are rather dear to us), and to feel that we are being conned into seeing *our* reality twisted to suit *his* view of it is a bit much.

Like politicians, writers make themselves unpopular when they fail to find an acceptable way of dressing up unpalatable truths. Indeed, the extent to which the arena is political can be measured more than any self-consciously political theatre by the offence which is taken when audiences feel their own 'sense of the world' to be violated by that of the author.

This same political quality is the key to its enormous democratic potential. Actors and audience are all physically present during a play's presentation, and even the audience, through its shufflings and murmurings, laughter and intentness, contributes actively to the persuasiveness of the illusion. What gets you the audience's vote is not how right you are, not how real you are, but how well you put over your sense of the world, whether it strikes sufficient chords of affinity with the audience for them to go along with you.

This is the true key to real characterisation – the politician's, as it were, rather than the voter's. Although the focus of audiences, and certainly of actors, is invariably on individual characters, the writer's feeling for character relates willy-nilly back to the overall 'sense of the world' in the play. A realistic tramp has no place on a fantasy park-bench unless it's *The Twilight Zone*. Mr Spock has no place in *Coronation Street* unless it's a comedy sketch (probably with Russ Abbott).

Note, however, that it isn't entirely impossible to conceive of Mr Spock in *Coronation Street*. So much depends on where the focus of the piece lies. If it wanted to say something about our expectations of social custom or modern myths, the juxtaposition could be extremely well chosen. Nothing demonstrates better the inextricable nature of the relationship between situation, plot and character. One springs from and is totally inconceivable without the other. Within his 'sense of the world' it is the playwright's sense of character which lends each protagonist and antagonist its appropriate force within the overall conflict.

Inside or outside

For some writers this means 'getting inside the character's skin' and expecting both actors and audience to follow suit; for others it means viewing characters from the outside, creating a distance between the way they behave and the audience's perception of them, so that the 'play' is one of ideas. These are two distinct tendencies in characterisation, and it's wise to know when one is operating which.

All plays take their material from real life and make something different from it, but in some the representation of reality is more important, while in others what's made of it is the uppermost consideration. Both approaches have their benefits, but their methods are quite distinct.

A play which is fundamentally presenting an argument is likely to know what it thinks of its characters before it starts. They are part of the intellectual schema of the play. It's popular to disparage this approach (when it's noticed), but it's both much more prevalent than people generally appreciate, and it can be great fun when handled well.

As observed earlier, we tend to accept 'interpretation' when it conforms to our own prejudices and accept it as real but reject it if it challenges them. There is, after all, nothing inherently wrong in the 'play' of a piece of theatre being the play of ideas. As much invention, wit and originality can be brought to bear on this form as any other – think of Stoppard, Dario Fo, Shaw – and it is no more demeaning for an actor to play a witty idea than a boring 'reality'.

The real danger lies in believing you're working one method when in fact you're working the other. This can either be writing a character purely from outside observation, but under the assumption it's 'real' (then wondering why an actor who can't get under its skin and the audience who aren't persuaded think it's phoney), or writing a character so real to you and true to your own personal feeling that the 'something different you make of it' is obscure (then wondering why no actor or audience can make sense of it).

I have to own up that, implicit in these observations, is the personal belief that the summit of playwriting achievement is a seamless combination of both methods. I certainly believe that in Shakespeare at his best one is both utterly persuaded of the reality of human behaviour presented, while at the same time absolutely sure of its place within the master's intellectual construct.

This isn't, however, just a matter of one playwright's approach as against another's. Different kinds of characterisation can sometimes occur within the same play. Just as an intense focus on a central character can sometimes lead to under-writing of subsidiary characters, so the playwright's intellectual sympathies can lead to certain characters being written from the inside while others remain externally or satirically observed. As an audience we become acutely aware that one character is, as it were, the comedian, for whom the other is the stooge.

Even this can work if the 'voice' of the play is loud and clear enough, if the passion or humour of the play is strong enough to take us with it. But it's a common failing, even among established writers, and I suspect that it's part and parcel of the white heat of a creative burst. Even so, it's as well to be aware from the outset – and certainly when you're rewriting – how easily you can slip from one mode to the other. After all, different kinds of characterisation suggest different worlds, and nothing is more irritating for an audience than not knowing which world it's supposed to be in.

How you look at it

Once again the relation of character to plot provides something of a clue to how this can happen. In the general run of characters' progress through a play, it can be expected that the experiences they go through will effect a change in them. Indeed, it is part of our expectations about cause and effect and the role of time in drama that characters do undergo change. If they don't, it's because of some stubborn streak. But it's equally possible that it's not the character which changes, rather our perception of it.

For example, it's possible you might set off with the idea of, say, a sympathetic character, but the more you expose her to the outside world of different situations and other characters, the more you realise she's a chump. Imperceptibly your character has changed from heroine to anti-heroine. As you have worked through your idea and learned more from the total situation, so your sympathy for the character has dwindled and the distance between you and her has increased.

Having completed a first draft in this manner, you may then realise that you've got a different character at the end of the play from the one at the beginning – and it's not that she's been changed by experience so much as that our view of her has altered by virtue of the situation. It's worth noting that a playwright like Brecht, capable of both complex characterisation and a fierce intellectual rigour, can go down a comparable road to this with Mother Courage, and yet create a consistent and convincing character.

Balanced forces

The problem for lesser talents comes when, far from being consistent, the audience's perception of the character is squeezed or tugged and pulled to fit into an inadequate plot-scheme. Equally dangerous, though less widely recognised, is when identification with the force of a character expands and grows till it overruns the balance of conflict within the plot.

The danger here – of an idealised view of the world in which the sheer will of an individual can dominate all situations – should be self-evident. Yet this kind of identification, fallacious though it is, remains a popular form of fantasy for writers, actors and audiences alike. Indeed, where it coincides with conformist perception – like Hollywood's perpetual production-line of rags-to-riches boxing champs, show-biz stars and tough-but-honest cops – it can even be considered 'real'. Before we Brits scoff, we should consider our own tradition of roguishly hypocritical, eccentrically bigoted and quizzically conforming charmers.

One way in which the idealised progress of the dominating single character can be challenged is when the forces of protagonist and antagonist are ranged in a situation where they're given equal weight. Throughout drama in general this is the commoner and certainly more dramatically interesting situation. The stronger one's sense of characters – in the plural and appearing through the whole play – the more difficult it becomes to force them through a super-ficially constructed plot. Not only will they, in the improvisational process of writing, develop sides to them which may make it impossible for you to 'have your way with them', but they will also begin to have an effect *on each other*.

Chicken and egg

In this sense the autonomy of the arena is being utilised to the full. What your characters do to each other and how they react to each other is, in this case, almost impossible to plan in any detail. Your 'sense of character' is then tested fiercely against the plot (your 'sense of the world'), as your imagination improvises their actions out there in that neutral zone between you and your audience. Pretty soon it becomes impossible even for you to tell which came first – a plot idea or the aspect of character linked to it.

Without a very sure sense of your characters, or a sound sense of the parameters of your plot, this can become bewildering. But the sense of danger and risk involved will, if successfully resolved, communicate to the audience. The openness of the means to your end will ensure a vivacity that the dead hand of overinterpretation or of idealistic identification can never achieve.

This consummation of character and plot relates back directly to the particular conflict the playwright wishes to expose, and to the functions which different characters perform in the playing out of that conflict. Antigone would be just a sister and Creon just a king without the conflict between them which draws out their characters. Even the psychologically more complex characters of Shakespeare are drawn out through what they do and their interplay with each other: Othello and Iago, Brutus and Cassius, Macbeth and Lady Macbeth, and so on.

In other words, action is the principal definer of character in a play, and whether it's St Joan arguing with the Dauphin or a blancmange arguing with a jelly about who's the tougher, context and conflict must be the writer's first considerations. It's almost impossible to have a character in a vacuum and, if you do, very difficult (*pace* Sam Beckett) not to make them boring.

Caricature or star?

It's important to emphasise this because so much of 20th-century drama has focused on the individual – from Hedda Gabler and Galileo to Jimmy Porter and The Singing Detective - that much of our popular thinking is directed towards seeing characters as individuals alone. The star system in films and commercial theatre, as well as much of actors' training, reinforces the same emphasis. But, just as situation and conflict define characters in the first instance, so it is what they do, the decisions they make, and only lastly what they say, that determines their significant development. And for all the characters, mentioned above, the forces ranged against them are considerable.

Clearly the more characters are on stage, the more they do and say, the more they interact with other characters, the richer they become. But this is purely a matter of air-time. It is nonsense to compare Hamlet with Rosencrantz (or was until Tom Stoppard) as a 'great character', but it's equally foolish to worry about the relative strength of Alison (as against Jimmy Porter) in *Look Back in Anger*. The interest of the play, the world of the play, is all in the central character's reactions, physical and verbal, to the world around him. As in *Mother Courage*, there is one protagonist, and all the other characters serve to draw out different sides of the conflict inherent in that figure.

If your basic interest in writing a play is in a particular individual who somehow sums up a conflict you feel particularly strongly about, no amount of attempting to make the other characters well rounded or three-dimensional will have any effect – except possibly to muddle and confuse the emotional dynamic of the play. By the same token, writing lengthy studies of a particular character – what they have for breakfast, what socks they wear, and so on – is useless unless it serves the principal conflict.

What an audience responds to finally is the *feel* of a character. Even the crassest caricature can win over hearts and minds if it is entertaining or corresponds to the way society at a particular time views a particular type. Who would argue with the portrayal of a train-driver as a lazy, slovenly, bolshie, egocentric bastard during the first winter snowfall when, regular as clockwork, the whole British transport system grinds to a halt? In more rational moments we might recognise that train-drivers are not to blame, that they listen to Beethoven and give blood, but at that particular time we see only the caricature in life, so we're quite prepared to accept it in fiction. If we share the feelings of the author, we'll go along with anything; if we don't, we need to be persuaded.

For the playwright then it's important to get to know the feel of a character. Even if the character is to appear only in a short scene and – like the bus conductor we see only once a day and always in the same situation – will therefore be only sketchily characterised, it's important that our sense of him is sure. And much of that sense will be determined by the force he represents in the action of the play.

From this kernel of feeling about a character a whole gamut of emotions may eventually spring, but that basic sense is important, not least because it is the guide to the consistency of character which will be so important to keep the audience orientated within the concerns of the play.

Character as mask

Mask exercises were introduced to the Royal Court Writers Group while I was still at school; these were developed for actors but offered to the group at that time by Keith Johnstone, and they had a profound influence on my own sense of characterisation – I know they helped other playwrights as well. In these exercises you put on a commedia-type half mask and look in a mirror. Immediately the face you see makes your body feel different and then begins to motivate you to move, breathe, do and speak in a manner over which your conscious control is irrelevant. I've encountered no exercise more valuable when it comes to making writers know what it feels like to be inside a character, to be driven by an inexorable force, to be limited by given characteristics but at the same time to be liberated to do things your real self would otherwise never do.

Writers' imaginations may try to liberate characters to enable them to live up to their fantasies, but they also need a powerful sense of their characters' limitations if they are not to slip into the kind of facile manipulation that offends the audience's sense of its own valued existence.

This is the root of that consistency in characterisation which is so necessary, not in order to make a character seem real, but to let the audience know where it stands within the action of the play, and then be in a position to judge its arguments.

As with the masks, every step the character takes, every gesture it makes, every line it utters, is like a building block added to the last. As one follows the other, proceeding from that initial sense, so the life of the character grows and the world of the play, your 'stage reality', is established bit by bit. Inconsistency of character, however true to life, unravels that web of illusion. It feels like cheating. Masks are not only a useful exercise for this, they are a wonderful symbol. It is the way a character is seen, more than what it essentially is, that determines its effect. Reception means more than transmission.

To sum up then, characters and action are inseparable. Whether your plot makes a character do something inconsistent with what we know of it so far, or whether your character forces a situation inconsistent with the world of the play, the dependency of one on the other is inviolable – unless you intend a kind of shock effect. This can be a perfectly legitimate device – to shake the audience out of a clichéd response, upset cosy expectations, make an unconventional connection or draw attention to what will be a significant new development.

But, such is the anticipation of cause leading to effect within the dramatic progression of a play, that deeds or utterances which occur without the ground having been prepared for them invariably require a subsequent and retrospective explanation. I'll go into this more later; sufficient to say for now that this will tend to hold up the momentum of the action. And this is where questions of structure become important.

7
Shaping up

Although the notion of the well-made play with its neatly arranged beginning, middle and end is now a thing of the past, structure remains one of the principal problems which bedevil playwrights. Because events unfold in the here and now before our eyes – not in a vague past where their exact chronology and exactly 'who knows what and when' can be fudged – their sequence can be crucial. Moving an event from one scene and placing it elsewhere, whether earlier or later, can have untold and peculiar consequences.

Houses of cards

Say you solve the problem of your central character's discovering corruption too late by moving the discovery forward. You may then have the problem of leaving his adversary's story relatively undeveloped. Not only that but the rhythm of the play overall – the pace at which the story is unfolding – becomes disrupted. Finally settling for a compromise which accounts for all these problems, you then realise you've lost what until now had been the delightful dramatic irony of the audience's being in the know about the corruption when your hero wasn't. Your whole house of cards collapses.

The difficulty with this kind of logistic manoeuvring is what Aristotle calls 'necessary progression' – that each part of a play is directly connected with the next – whether you like it or not. In changing one thing for the better, it seems something else is almost certain to change for the worse. The exercise of even attempting the change can become daunting. You end up going round in circles, like looking for the loose end in a tangled skein of wool.

Sometimes, however, you can have the feeling that a plot ought to unlock, but you simply haven't found the hidden key yet. Recognising where the main action of a play lies, which of the characters are the principal ones around which it revolves and, above all, where the audience's attention will be directed, can go a long way to solving this.

That means it's back to the scenario. Many of the problems of structure can be solved in advance by the kind of sound planning which ensures that the momentum of the play remains focused on its central concerns. Even so, there can still be pleasing twists and ironies which you've uncovered while writing and which you're loath to lose. It then becomes a matter of looking at a particular scene and relating it to the overall development of the play. 'If Character A finds out about the corruption here, what are the consequences for Character B?' 'How does that affect the pace of the plot?' 'How will it change the audience's perception of the whole?'

Who you know and what you know

In struggling with this, it pays to think about the trajectory of each character's development: where is it coming from and where is it going? The less you've fudged the answer to these questions, the easier it is to decide at what point in that development you can introduce a change. If you know what a character wants at each moment in the play, it becomes a lot easier to decide where the new element you wish to introduce will work to best effect.

In this connection thought is a vital component to the dramatic interest of a play. It's not a quality you hear a lot about in run-of-the-mill discussion of theatre; passion is the quality people notice and respond to more readily. Yet every great performance in theatre possesses moments where, without the character's saying anything, you know what's in their mind. For an actor to have something to play, the playwright must have put it there.

It is crucial then that the playwright has at least an inkling of what this is – the character's thoughts as well as feelings. And thought becomes even more important when it comes to what a character knows at any point in a story. Knowledge, after all, can make for the difference between guilt and innocence, contrivance and spontaneity, accident and intent.

The terror of the blank page

With all these questions rattling round in your head, choosing where to start a play, or even a scene, can seem an insuperable task. The 'terror of the blank page' afflicts all writers, and it's often better if the action is so clear in one's mind that a scene writes itself. But not always. Sometimes our unconscious borrowing from the plethora of drama around us or misguided notions of 'a good place to start' can set us off on the wrong foot before we've begun.

Translated from the Irish, this means a good scene can come into your head, one which is indeed fine in itself but would actually belong far better in another play, or in the same play but in a different position. And it's not only inspiration which can be misleading. It can also be that rather plodding, literal-minded rationality which tells you to go back to the very beginning - a character's childhood, the first meeting between lovers, whatever - when in fact you could reveal just as much and make it far more interesting if you started the story in, as it were, midstream.

In fact it's often better if a play starts just after the beginning of its story-line. If something has happened before the first scene, the opening situation is already a result of a developing action. In this way we are immediately plunged into the main action of the play through the characters' reactions to that initial event. This means that the plot is already under way when we join it, so that for the audience it's like jumping on to a moving bus.

If events are already moving ahead, exposition of setting, characters and story can take place simultaneously through the characters' reactions to what is happening, rather than having to be laboriously described in words. First scenes which wind up the story like a piece of old clockwork, setting the scene or painstakingly introducing us to the characters, are invariably unnecessary. Indeed, exposition of setting and characters through dialogue alone can be a dangerous business, leading to stilted Ibsenesque lines similar to those parodied by Stoppard in *The Real Inspector Hound*:

> MRS DRUDGE [*answering the phone*]: Hello, the drawing-room of Lady Muldoon's country residence one morning in early spring?

Sometimes dialogue alone *can* do the trick. After all, theatre dialogue is active, unlike the passivity of television dialogue. This is very much a matter of theatrical style. It's not a familiar approach, but the blunt, verbal exposition of Brecht's 'outfront' *Lehrstuck* style gets us immediately into the characters' dilemma, and therefore into the tensions of the play – in this case *The Mother*:

> VLASOVA: I'm almost ashamed to offer my son this soup.

But even here action is paramount. The Mother is hesitating. By showing her feelings and indicating the tension in the relationship with her son, the wider, social context of the play is quickly opened up.

And it is true of plays generally that more will be indicated about character, setting and plot through what characters do than through what they say. This also gives you the opportunity to set the ball of your plot rolling immediately, rather than stealthily 'introducing' the story-line at some point later, after you've painstakingly introduced the characters.

The answer is to think of an initial action as the core of your opening scene which simultaneously sets the situation in terms of time and place, introduces the characters and kick-starts the principal conflict of your story-line. Once again I should emphasise that this action need not be physical or external. It can be a mother hesitating. The point is simply that it presents us with an event or situation which introduces us immediately to the heart of the play's conflict. If we think back to the idea of the main action as the spine of your play, what happens in your first scene should be the first vertebra which leads to all the others.

The best example of this is the beginning of *King Lear*. Look it up if you don't remember. Within two lines the fact of the king's dividing up his realm is announced; within two pages he has begun to do it – he has already decided to set his daughters a task, they respond to this task in their various ways – and the die for the rest of the play is cast. The first action is the one from which all subsequent actions proceed. Through it we are introduced to the characters, the situation and the 'world of the play'. By the end of the scene we are keen to know what'll happen next – helped, of course, by Goneril's cliff-hanger line:

We must do something, and i' th' heat.

Their actions follow his, the effect, as it were, of his cause, which in turn causes others to follow. Immediately the dynamic of the play is established.

Not everyone can be Shakespeare of course, and the perfect beginning may perhaps come easier when your play is based on a good old standby fairy story. Nor do the events at the beginning need to be as momentous as dividing up a kingdom. But it's better if they're central to the eventual plot.

Not only do we know exactly where we stand in *King Lear*, but we are intrigued to know what happens next. Orientated within the world of the play through that initial central event, we now await the consequences. That initial situation has acted as a focal point, providing a setting, indicating themes, revealing character and propelling all of them forward simultaneously.

If this sounds a somewhat helter-skelter approach to beginnings, then it flatly contradicts the other golden rule concerning them, which is that they should be slow. An audience takes in a great deal of data within the first ten minutes of watching a play, much of it visual, and too much information, coming too thick and fast, can lead to confusion or the loss of important pointers. Pace can be a matter of production rather than script, but it does no harm to think selectively about what it's absolutely necessary to know at the beinning and about the speed at which it unfolds.

This selectivity can also help to clarify what the central concern of your play actually is, clearing away some of the interesting, but secondary, byways which may accompany it. You can always explore these byways later – if the momentum of your main action allows it. Trying to fit in interesting but basically irrelevant data at any stage can disturb the main dynamic of a play, not to mention the audience's focus on what really matters. Ultimately it can lead to the kind of tangle described at the beginning of this chapter.

Even if you look at it from a purely commercial point of view, your first five pages will need to make clear and compulsive reading if they're to motivate the overburdened director or literary manager of a theatre to read beyond them.

Every scene a crossroads

Much of what applies to the opening scene of a play applies to every other scene along the way. The sense of movement through time is crucial, so it's always valuable to think of what has happened before and after a scene. It's as if the trajectory of development of each character is like a stratum of rock, and the choice of where scenes begin and end is like taking a cross-section through it, so that you can, in a sense, read the development of a character back and forward from each individual scene. (I'm using the word 'scene' here as I did when talking about scenarios: a segment of the play's action centred around a particular event or development.)

To achieve this sense of movement through time – like the idea of a first scene being a moving bus – the playwright needs to have some idea of what his characters have done or were doing before the scene starts – 'where they've come from'. Similarly we should have some sense at the end of the scene (as with Regan and Goneril) of what they'll do next, 'where they're going'. In this respect each scene is like a crossroads – one character coming along one path, another coming along another; they meet at the point of the scene, have an influence upon each other and then go off in yet another direction. *Waiting for Godot* is a whole play built on this principle, set literally at a crossroads.

Much of this can be achieved through thinking about motivation. What does this character want? What are they hoping to get out of this encounter with another character? Is their meeting casual or accidental? Or is it intentional – in which case, who set it up? And why? These questions will be vital to the actor playing the part, who needs to know exactly what he's doing in the scene; and they're vital to the playwright concerned to carry his audience along with him. If conflict is to do with a clash of wills, then the hopes, wishes and intentions of characters at every point in the play's development play a vital part in its forward momentum.

Spinning plates

Even more important, as far as the structure of the play is concerned, is that the specific conflict of a scene, the site of each particular crossroads, is in some way connected to the central conflict of the whole play and carries it forward. Problems of structure frequently arise when new scenes or unexpected developments accrue around, say, the story-line of a particular character, but these take the play further and further away from its original focus. It is the *central* conflict, the one announced in the first scene, that the audience needs to remain in touch with, not just the side of it represented by a particular character, however interesting that character may be.

Unlike the author of a popular 19th-century novel, you can't afford to take your public off on an extended detour into the background or fate of an individual character and pick up the threads of your main plot later. Because a play happens in the here and now over a span of about two hours, every development is significant, as is every gesture, and so every strand of plot needs to be kept alive in the audience's mind, if its sudden revival later on is not to come as a jolt.

Timing is also vital. A play can establish its own sense of time in an audience's mind, whether the gap between scenes is years or minutes, but, once established, an expectation has been set up. In a play where months pass between the scenes, suddenly juxtaposing a scene which takes place hours after the previous one will upset the rhythm. This may be what you want – if it happens around a critical moment in the plot, that's fine – but otherwise it will upset the audience's sense of time-keeping in the 'world of the play' and possibly distract them from the issue that's important to you.

Keeping the important ingredients of a play's central interest alive, whether these are its characters, a strand of the story or its sense of time, is not unlike a juggler spinning plates. Nothing is accidental, remember. Each ingredient, once set in motion, needs to be returned to and touched on regularly, if it's to be kept in play till the end. A loose end, neglected, will wobble in the audience's mind, as those plates do before they fall, and become a fierce distraction.

This is particularly true where the play's central interest focuses on more than two characters. Much contemporary drama still relies on engagement with its central concerns through identification with a single, central character or, sometimes, the conflict between two opposing characters. Much of modern life however, at work and in leisure activities, takes place in broader, social groups. From factory work to the parent-teacher association to the squash club, more and more of our lives are taken up with group activities.

Neither our expectations of drama nor, unfortunately, dramatists' skills have really caught up with this change. Conflict is still seen mainly as something between just two characters. Think of the vast number of scenes where the axis of conflict is between two people, and the relatively tiny number where three or more are involved.

In television, series like *Lou Grant*, *Casualty* and *NYPD Blue* are distinctive in their ability to locate individual story-lines within a broader social structure, but even then each week tends to focus on one particular character, or one character's story at a time. Plays like Wesker's *The Kitchen* or David Storey's *The Changing Room* or my own *Female Transport* are in this respect the exception rather than the rule, and yet so much of what happens in our lives is the result of collective, rather than individual, social pressure.

And just as organising a meeting between three people as opposed to two can mean three phone-calls rather than one, so scenes where three or more characters are involved quickly increase the number of relationships to be borne in the dramatist's mind. The spinning plates multiply.

In this situation, for actors as well as audience, a new kind of dynamic then comes into play. No longer is identification with a particular individual or the conflict between two the point of focus; rather it becomes a matter of engagement with the *situation* as a whole. It is not only the characters individually but also the development of their shared situation which has to be kept spinning. To remove, as it were, a particular character from this collective situation and develop his or her story alone implies a disruption of that focus. Either the play is about this group and their situation together, or it is about an individual. The audience's engagement with the momentum of the group situation, even if it's only three people, has to be taken into account.

Just as the setting of a play can become as important as a principal character in determining how an audience perceives a play, so the common plight of a group of characters, once established, cannot be ignored as the play progresses. It's a more complicated unity than any mentioned by Aristotle and, born of the modern age, it remains a relatively rare one, but it has its own internal logic like the rest.

What's at stake?

Part of the reason for the scarcity of collective or group drama is no doubt due to the economic pressure towards small casts. But it is also a failing not only of dramatists but also of newspaper and broadcasting journalists that they understand and play to identification with the personal and individual, encouraging and developing it, while leaving significant areas of more social intercourse unexplored.

It's fascinating to speculate about the possible social consequences of this neglect – the loner mass murderer, the growth of various kinds of group therapies, etc. - but one of the consequences for drama is that both playwrights and audiences can have extreme difficulty in identifying and retaining the focus of a scene where three or more characters are in play.

One way of ensuring that a scene holds a genuine dramatic interest of its own is simply to ask 'What's at stake here?' What is the point of issue between the characters? Who wants what, and what are their various attitudes towards the main issue? Above all – and this is what one hopes will hold the audience – what will be the outcome? If the suspense of that question can have the audience on the edge of their seats, and if the situation is one which links back to the main conflict and themes of the play, then each scene will be advancing the main action, however many characters it contains.

This applies to two-handed scenes as well, indeed any scene, but it becomes particularly apposite in scenes with three or more characters. If a group of people are in a particular situation, whatever their individual backgrounds and desires, there is usually some common concern which one way or another affects them all. To keep the dramatic interest of the scene alive, it is that common element, not only the individual fates of the characters, which needs to be borne in mind. Often it is by combining the two, by revealing the collective fate through the individual and vice versa, that interest in the story as a whole and the particular interest in an individual character can be maintained.

Public speaking

A common difficulty for playwrights is that they become so interested in a particular tussle between, say, a pair of characters, that they forget that all the other characters are on stage. It is not enough to say to yourself 'Oh, Character C is reading a newspaper and Character D is filing her nails'. These characters will retain an active presence in the scene whether they're actually speaking or not. Even if it's only as an 'ear' which the other characters have to be aware of, it's important to know why they're there, why they don't just push off, and what their feelings are towards the main protagonists of the scene.

In this sense the playwright has to be aware of the situation not only of each character on stage, but also of the collective vibrations between them. It is out of this group alertness that the general dynamic of a scene with several characters present will emerge. It is the sum of all their different reactions, and how that relates to their common predicament, which will create the interest of the scene.

It's important therefore to bear in mind how each character will *hear* the others and react to what they do, as well as how playing to the other characters as an audience will condition what they say and do. People couch what they have to say differently, according to the ear of those present. At the end of *Who's Afraid of Virginia Woolf?*, for example, Martha cannot openly admit to George, in front of Nick and Honey, that the son which he has just pronounced dead is a figment of her imagination. So she uses phrases like 'I won't let you do this' and 'You can't decide these things', coded phrases which George understands but which initially baffle Nick and Honey.

In all forms of group situation, a kind of public speaking is involved. Whether it's the formal jargon of a committee, or the life and soul of the party at the local pub, there is a sense in which characters in these situations play directly to the arena, that third space between author and audience. Moreover, the other characters forming their stage audience and the real audience become all one. Here the situation begins to creep towards audience participation of an unusual kind, for the position of the real audience is almost identical to that of the onlookers in the play. Indeed, working-class people, used to being amongst large groups at work and play, and even sometimes at home, can get very directly involved in this kind of situation. In performances of my play with Paul Thompson, *The Motor Show*, Ford workers would recognise certain situations in the play and call out as if taking part in a real event.

Two sides do not a conflict make

It's more than possible that something you thought was a conflict when you planned your scenario turns out, in the writing of it, to be nothing of the sort. You may, for example, have thought 'I'll bring A and B together in this scene, and they'll argue about such-and-such'. Whether your sense of the conflict between the two characters was sharper when you were planning, or whether you simply haven't given the situation enough thought, it may well turn out to be a dull, flat scene in which the two have nothing more than a rather boring conversation.

In this situation it's imperative to bear in mind that simple disagreement does not constitute a conflict. Many plays simply present rows, in which attitudes are revealed, but in which there is no development or movement. The test of whether a scene with an argument is essentially dramatic is to ask whether the characters are using their arguments to some end or purpose. Whether to persuade or dissuade, undermine or overpower the other character, the important issue is whether they are trying to *do* something with their line of argument, affect or influence the other character towards some goal. Like every line being a gesture, it's important to ask what their intentions are behind their disagreement. What are they up to?

If you find this question difficult to answer, it may be that you haven't thought enough about where the characters are coming from, the urgency of their situation, their hopes and desires; or it may be that the scene leads nowhere, isn't developing, its characters aren't going anywhere. This is the time to try and stand outside yourself and ask if it's a real conflict. Do the characters have a momentum of their own outside your will as a writer? Or have you just put them on stage so that you can spout? Is the dialogue representing their urgency? Are we learning something new from every line, is each line advancing the action, or are you simply letting them ramble? Is there really something at stake?

The volleyball net

The idea of characters as forces comes into play here again, as does the question of a character's consistency. The tension of a scene is often dependent on the extent to which the wills of the characters are well established. Like a volleyball net strung between two poles, the firmer the poles are rooted, the greater the tension in the net. If the dramatic force of your characters is well grounded and the difference between their desires is clear, the tension between them will be self-evident.

For this you not only have to be sure of their motivation, but that what they stand for in a particular scene is consistent with the knowledge we have of them so far. It only takes one of your characters to be wobbly – either vague in its aspirations or contradictory in what we've perceived about it up till now – for its pole to be uprooted and the net to collapse.

Of course, it isn't always easy to define where the tension of a scene lies – particularly if it's to do with the complex, inner effect which one character has upon another. But most kinds of tension boil down to three basic possibilities.

The first is external or physical: A wants B to do something (i.e. leave the room) – the tension lies in whether she will or not, and the result is obvious. The second is internal to one or more characters: A wants B to love him – here the resolution is more ambiguous and may not be resolved physically but in a change of attitude. The third kind lies outside the characters present on stage: A and B wait to hear the price of British Telecom shares. (Once again *Waiting for Godot* supplies an example of an entire play built on this principle.)

In the resolution of all these conflicts there is a sense of 'being brought to': B is brought to leave the room; A is brought to the realisation that B doesn't love him; A and B are brought to the realisation they've been sold a pup. Look at what the characters are being 'brought to' in the course of a scene, and you have a clearer idea of where the scene is going. Look at this scene by scene, and you have a clearer idea of where the whole play is going.

Once you've identified exactly where the tension of a scene lies, it's easier to tell how well it relates to and advances your main theme, or whether it's an interesting detour about one of the characters which you'll regret later as all your other plates stop spinning and crash to the floor. This becomes particularly important as you approach the end and look back to see if all your loose ends are tied up, and whether you've arrived at the destination you were aiming for.

Means to ends

One of the commonest mistakes made by novice playwrights is that they end their plays ponderously. I suspect that this is the result of getting in a stew about them – the feeling that not enough has been said, or that the play so far hasn't quite clinched what it set out to achieve. This can lead to heavily overwritten last scenes and extremely symbolic last lines. Sometimes it becomes the dramatic equivalent of a Beethoven coda, with several seeming endings, crescendos, dyings away and 'final' chords before the actual end.

The first remedy for this is to try not to get in a stew about them. The chances are the audience has actually cottoned on to what you were saying, and that repeating it several times is merely irritating. The second remedy is to bear in mind that once again it will be what *happens* last, rather than that sonorous last line, which will stick in people's minds. In *Who's Afraid of Virginia Woolf?*, for example, we may not remember that the penultimate line is the title of the play, but we're more likely to remember that George destroys Martha's fantasy about their son.

It's even possible that the feeling you sometimes get of not having clinched the ending is due to having found an action but not the right action for the ending – that final vertebra in the chain, connected and relating back to those which have gone before. Simply having someone die, or kill someone, or leave the room, or go to bed, can be a cop-out. Nor will any amount of mere speech necessarily satisfy an expectation aroused in an earlier scene, or a loose end of a character's development which you've failed to tie up.

The third remedy is a happier one. The wonderful thing about last scenes is that they're the only scenes where you don't have to worry about what happens next, where the characters are going. It may well be that the playwright's last gesture is to send his characters off to new pastures, but, having done that, he's shot of them. It's almost a way of defining endings which otherwise, given the inordinate range of possibilities, is impossible to do. Above all, it suggests the sense of letting go which is important to the dramatist, if to no one else. I have frequently stopped working on a last scene, reaching what seems like a temporary block and thinking I have much further to go, and then realised that I have in fact finished. The sense of relief is not to be spurned.

This ability to let go can apply at any point in a play. I'm often asked whether I think endings should be optimistic or pessimistic. There is, of course, no 'should be' about it. Just as characters may receive the transmitted will of other characters differently from the way they're expected to, so an audience cannot be guaranteed to respond to receive the transmitted message of a playwright. Audiences will take and leave from a play exactly what suits them. Overstatement of a particular theme may well act like an aversion therapy on an audience. The contrivance of an optimistic ending in the face of horrific events may well reinforce an audience's pessimism, and vice versa. If the evidence is there, the judgement will be self-evident.

Retrospective explanation

A similar problem can occur at any point in a play where a play-wright feels he's left something out, not emphasised something enough, or needs to insert some vital information about a character but hasn't yet found the active way to do so. Sometimes there is a recourse to monologue, sometimes the anecdotal telling of a story which happened in the past, sometimes even a flashback. Almost always such moments come as a huge hold-up in the forward momentum of the play. Nothing demonstrates better the need for everything in drama to be shown as a product of action and conflict than this kind of tedious retrospective explanation.

It can even happen over a relatively short span of dialogue where, say, a character does something out of the blue and then, because it's so unexpected or out of character, explains why they did it. It often happens because of an instinctive feeling by the playwright that a character should react in a particular way to the situation in hand. Its whole point is that it's unexpected so it can't be built towards, yet it's still got to be explained.

The contrast between the suddenness of the reaction and the tedium of the explanation in these instances says much about the way drama needs to proceed. The sense of one action following another like temporal building blocks, of cause and effect, of logical sequence, prevails – even if your desire is to explode the conventionalism of this as a view of life.

The point here is that, in order to convey an aspect of the inner life of a character or describe an event in the past, the audience needs to know about through a lengthy monologue or duologue, the dramatist needs to have 'bought' the time that such a break in the forward momentum of the play represents.

A tension needs to have been built up, a head of steam, so that, when it comes, the explanation of past events, inner feelings or simple musing, is seen to have a cause, an urgency of its own and, above all, is justified within the pressing demands of the here and now. This comes to be increasingly relevant towards the end of a play and is perhaps a measure of how successfully the dramatic impetus of the piece has built to the point where it occurs.

Committing to memory

Connected with this, and contributing to the sense of finality about endings, is the quality of memory. There remains still – in spite of more than a decade of shock endings, abrupt endings, slice-of-life endings which just halt and (that favourite of the mid-20th-century moral vacuum) the inconclusive ending – a desire in audiences to recap the events of the whole play, to hark back to the beginning, touch on moments throughout the play and try to grasp it all as a whole.

It's interesting that in film and television, as a way of making more palatable the execrable practice of putting what are virtually actors' publicity photos besides the final credits, they sometimes show stills of the action. If you've enjoyed the film or programme, this can even offer quite a pleasant recall.

I'm not suggesting that playwrights indulge in lengthy speeches recalling every sentimental incident in the play, but it can be very satisfying if the final action of a play somehow pulls together and echoes previous events. Even an exact repeat of a line earlier in the play, spoken again under the different circumstances at the end of the play, can work as an ironic reminder of all that has happened in the meantime. Once again, like striking middle C on a piano with the sustaining pedal depressed and hearing the vibration of all the other Cs, the connectedness of a last scene to the other vertebrae can lend the play a satisfying wholeness.

8
On second thoughts

Rewriting, or editing, one's work is necessarily a more rational activity than creating an initial draft. Already you are stepping back from the heat of actually forging the work and taking a cooler, more detached view. In looking at what you've done from, as it were, outside, you're immediately being a kind of audience to your own work.

In fact this process is also going on while you're writing your first draft – every time you stop and look back over what you've done so far. In this respect there is no such thing as a first draft, unless one maintains the discipline of not changing a word until the whole version is finished. Indeed, much of what this book has already said, in that it's essentially critical rather than creative, could strictly be said to apply to rewriting more than the more individual and elusive process of writing itself.

Standing over your own shoulder

Even so, there are distinct aspects of revision itself which are worth spending some time on. The first is that very quality of distance. This has much to do with writers being initially inside what they create, willing an effect, expressing an intention. The ability to stand outside that initial process, to judge the success of an effect and whether its intention is achieved, does not necessarily come as naturally as the first flow of dialogue. You need to be a kind of foreman to yourself, standing over your own shoulder.

For many writers the simple answer is to put a first draft away for a month or even longer, forget all about it, do something entirely different and come back to it with a fresh mind. Certainly this can make it easier to view things objectively. In this sense time is the most valuable commodity a writer can have. The more your work has been performed, the better you get to know your own special foibles, and the easier it becomes to spot possible dangers. But when you're starting you may need tricks to help you be stricter with yourself.

Many people start a process of revision with the firm resolve to change everything. The further you read into a draft, however, the more you can get tugged back into the frame of mind behind your original intentions. This isn't surprising, since presumably you still remain sympathetic to the work as a whole. Not only that, but the very fact that what you've already written exists, perhaps neatly typed in crisp black on white, lends it a certain established authority. Against that, any revision you may contemplate still requires the effort of actually writing it. It may well be that you need some other authority, whether the prospect of production, the opinion of a respected friend or sheer self-discipline, to wind yourself up to the task.

The first way of establishing an external discipline for yourself is to refer back to your synopsis, scenario and notes. Since these are also in black and white and are a clear indication of your intentions, they can represent an alternative authority and something perhaps to aim for. Beyond that, it's perhaps as well to restrict yourself to reading and working on only a few pages at a time, so that you're not too taken over by the momentum of the original – possibly even working over a particular scene several times before proceeding to the next.

This can get confusing in itself, since it's not uncommon to be in a slightly different frame of mind each time you work through. A crude but effective device for coming to terms with the vicissitudes of one's moods is simply to make your comments in a different colour each time you go through. If nothing else, it familiarises you with your own critical idiosyncrasies. Proceeding in this way from line to line through a scene at a time, one's sense of the immediacy of each moment on stage is sharpened. In this way many of the questions you need to ask yourself about the play are easier to put and ultimately, one hopes, easier to answer. There is no doubt, however, that reading back is a skill in itself, requiring a lot of self-discipline.

The cold shower

The simplest way of getting real distance at any stage in a script's progress is to show it to someone else. This is the 'cold shower' theory of self-criticism, for the results will almost certainly be surprising. For better or worse, this is the first chance you get to see your work as others see it, to find out whether what you're transmitting is being received. The deeper you're inside the work, the more fraught this self-revelation can be, and many prefer to do as much as they can alone before showing a script further.

On the one hand, revising alone has the advantage of seeing your own vision through as far as possible before any outside influence is brought to bear on it. Showing a draft before you've really clinched what you want to do with it can result in your intentions being knocked sideways by ignorant or insensitive comment before they've really crystallised. On the other hand, if you're in real difficulty, a sympathetic second opinion can help you find a way to crystallise an intention which you might have taken months to discover or indeed never discovered at all.

Of sharks and guinea-pigs

Besides these artistic considerations, there are unfortunately also commercial ones. Not the least of these is the danger of someone trying to muscle in on your idea. Whether a potential co-writer or director, there are always more than enough candidates who imagine that, for the price of a few hastily considered suggestions, they can cut themselves in on your copyright. That, of course, is a natural right, protected by law, and you need to be aware of it.

To many people in theatre, writing is an invisible and therefore mysterious skill. For these reasons it inspires both fear and envy. On the one hand, the power of the playwright's script can be seen as godlike, determining everything, and therefore resented; on the other hand the one-in-a-thousand, commercially successful play which earns a fortune in royalties is seen as money for old rope. Unlike the process of rehearsal, few have any inkling of the very special effort which goes into writing. They see only their own contribution in production and feel it's that which has 'made the play'.

Those of us lucky enough to have had plays produced twice know that, while a director's or actor's contribution is unique, it does not make the play. A line changed one way to help an actor in one production can be changed back for another equally unique actor in a second production.

The point here is that the special contribution of everybody involved in theatre production is part of a collaborative process in which each skill has its own responsibilities and privileges. Writers don't ask for a cut of directors' fees in return for their suggestions about casting or in rehearsal. Plays can make theatres' and actors' reputations, but writers don't ask for a percentage of the subsequent earnings of either. Writers are often only too acutely aware of the massive responsibility involved in having their 'baby' produced. They need also to be aware that their copyright is inviolable.

But, besides the dangers, the cold shower of getting an outside opinion can have real advantages. Whether your imagination is essentially stubborn and in need of a short, sharp shock, or whether your confidence is fragile and you seek confirmation of your highest hopes and worst fears, the very act of showing a script to someone else is the first stage of going public.

For some people the experience is comparable to that of the first read-through before a play is rehearsed. And for many playwrights the read-through is almost the equivalent of a first night for an actor. For the first time the work is no longer private. Currently, a few theatres offer the possibility of plays receiving public readings. In each of these situations your work is public for the first time and, in a very real sense, out of your hands. The truth is that each of these stages represents a progression towards full production and, as such, there is much to be learned from them.

Intention and effect

The first thing to acknowledge about trying your work out on someone is that whoever you choose as your guinea-pig, however near and dear, they are unlikely to share your preoccupations with the same intensity. Marriages and relationships have been put under considerable strain because this simple fact of life hasn't been recognised. Your intentions – what I have broadly described in the first chapter as your idea – now have to stand entirely according to their effect.

It's quite possible that, as you listen to feedback – whether it comes from a sympathetic individual or a public discussion – you are still so wrapped up in your intentions that you fail to hear quite useful information about their effect. It's as well to try to distance yourself from the start so that, whatever the response, you make the most use of it.

In this respect it's perhaps a good idea to make a note of how people have responded to a first draft, because it isn't always easy, immersed in your intentions as you are, to grasp the line of appraisal behind what another says at first hearing. It's only when you get back to rewriting, when you yourself are thinking critically, that the pertinence of people's fragmented comments can become apparent, revealing the effect the work's had on them.

The benefits and disadvantages of outside criticism function differently for different people. For some it's such a relief to be free of the lone responsibility of creation that they're prepared to believe and accept anything anyone says. For others what's gone into the writing is so complex and private, almost any comment will seem superficial and irrelevant. How such feedback is assimilated is ultimately more important than assuming one can import criticism wholesale into a work and transform it instantly.

Translating criticism

If you're lucky, a fresh eye on what you've done will solve that common dilemma of knowing something isn't quite right but not knowing exactly what or how. Someone else is much likelier to be able to identify the problem, though almost certainly not the solution. It's one thing to know something is wrong, even to have that sense confirmed; it's quite another to do something about it.

The latter is entirely the writer's responsibility. It may be a hard cross to bear, but ultimately there is no escape. You started this, it's down to you to finish it. No one else can know the piece as intimately as you, with all its intentions and the full implications of every line and gesture. Invariably one is thrown back on one's own resources to find a satisfactory remedy, not least because what others have said, however right about effects, may be totally off the point as far as your intentions are concerned. From this point of view every reaction, however fatuous, is valuable because it will tell you *something*. The difficulty lies in making sense of it all. It's you who will have to translate half-baked reactions, contradictory opinions and sincere but misguided comments into action.

Indeed the full progression of a play from idea in your head to performance before an audience is like a series of translations. First it's translated into your words, then it's translated into the voices and movements of actors, then it's translated into the audience's mind. At each stage it's almost inevitable (as they say of translation) that something will be lost. I remember seeing a fine West Indian play rendered into a pastiche of black folksiness in an attempt to make it 'commercial', in almost the same way that O'Casey's Dublin was popularised. It's no wonder, with so many layers of impression and expression to pass through, most of them dominated by middle-class English taste, that theatre remains such a conservative medium.

Given these translation difficulties, there is little difference between sympathetic and hostile criticism. Someone can warm to your subject, spot a problem but be quite misleading as to how to solve it. By contrast, someone who hates the whole thing may inadvertently, and for the wrong reasons, put their finger on the problem, and you immediately see how to resolve it.

In other words it's better to swallow one's pride or ego, ignore whether the response is sympathetic and, keeping it at arm's length, take from it what is useful to you. In the end, it is the writer who decides what stays in and what goes – for better and worse – so all criticism has finally to be assimilated. Whether it contributes to the final creative whole is finally decided by virture of whether you can 'translate' it, that is, reconcile it with your original intent.

You're on your own

Since all writers have their own bad writing habits (and most, including me, will flout many, if not all, the rules in this book at some time), the expression 'cold turkey' might be more apposite than 'cold shower' to describe the rigour of radical rewriting. One may certainly need to exert the most ruthless discipline on oneself simply to write, let alone rewrite, and at a certain point the two processes can seem synonymous (in adaptation, for example). While actually writing, however, you'd not get very far if you were constantly looking over your shoulder, anticipating criticism; in rewriting you need precisely that – to be your own severest critic.

First, you need to go back to the beginning and ask 'Does this really fulfil my original intention?' That can be the hardest nettle of all to grasp and may well imply going back to synopsis and scenario and seeing where you've strayed. It may even turn out that you prefer your wanderings to the straight and narrow of your plan but, before you can identify whether this is going to work all the way through, you'll need to change your plan. It's no good fudging and saying 'This strays off my plan but I like it, so that's OK', and then 'I don't like this, but it follows my plan so that's OK'. To anyone else it would sound as if you're writing two plays. So you'd need two plans. That old taskmaster, Choice, has reared its head again.

If you're not straying too far, the next question is whether each development in the play, its string of events or scenes, is really hitting the nail on the head. If your guinea-pigs have responded to parts of the play with comments which at first are quite incomprehensible to you, it could be that a scene is simply not communicating what you intended.

It can be very difficut indeed to get over this problem: you're seeing things one way, your try-out audience is seeing them another, and all the comment passing between you is at cross purposes. That's why it can be handy to distance yourself and put yourself in the other person's position, if only temporarily, in order to at least see the problem from outside. It's much more of an acute difficulty if you leave it till rehearsals, when there may be a dozen different perspectives to cope with.

This applies particularly to characterisation. Once a first draft is completed, you have a better idea of whether your characters, now fully developed, have that consistency as a force which makes their presence on stage a clear and active element in the story. Look at each scene and ask where the characters are coming from and where they're going. What is their motivation, their will? Are we constantly reminded of this, the conflict between them developing through each line? Do they sometimes sound the same, and is that just you thinking aloud, or is there a purpose behind it? Is the volleyball net firmly rooted in every scene?

Weeding

Once you've attended to the broader elements of the script – idea, structure, consistency of characterisation, and so on – you're down to the detail of gesture, whether through physical action or dialogue. This is where you need to ask 'Is this really necessary? Does it advance the action?' Much of what we write in a first draft is discovery. Like an improvisation, it seems less fresh the second time around, and there's a good chance that the means you've used to make your discovery is now redundant.

An excellent way to judge dialogue is, of course, to hear it read aloud. If you don't have the opportunity of hearing it read by others, then reading it aloud yourself can be nearly as instructive. For a start, you discover whether the lines are actually speakable, whether you've left tongue-twisters in or lines so long they're impossible to say in one breath.

But the main thing is not so much speaking the lines as *hearing* them. (One might add 'as others hear them'.) This gives you your strongest sense of whether your meaning is actually communicating. Personal syntax being so variable, you won't, without others reading your script, have the benefit of knowing whether a line constitutes the most lucid and accessible means of expressing a particular sentiment, but you will get some inkling of it. As you read, a quick wavy line underneath anything which sounds odd might be a way of indicating dialogue susceptible to later weeding.

A common practice in dialogue is to have one character asking the other feed questions such as 'What?', 'What d'you mean?', 'Really?' or simply 'Oh?' Sometimes a character will require another character to repeat what they've said: 'You mean, you actually. . ?', 'What I mean is. . .' and so on. Weed all this out. It's the playwright's equivalent of doodling. Look for where the interest of the dialogue is actually moved forward. What's the next thing somebody says which genuinely moves things on. It may be that the line will be stronger if it simply runs on without the feed.

Repetition is a big enemy, except where it's intentional and telling us something special about a character or situation. Sometimes repetition can build to become a dramatic effect in itself, but it's easy to kid yourself that a repetition is more interesting than it actually is. Weed out all meaningless repetition, whether in dialogue or situation – having somebody do something twice or more, simply because you can't think what else to have them do.

A good way of thinking about repetition is to remind yourself of the meaning of the phrase 'History never repeats itself'. The implication is that, as time moves on, circumstances change, so that exactly the same event can never happen twice. So it should be in a play.

Dialogue which reflects natural speech is often littered with the little phrases, like grace-notes in music, which ease the playwright (and sometimes the actor) into the meat of a line. 'Well,' to start a line, is number one in the Useless Phrases Hit Parade. 'Oh' at the start of a line is number two. 'Really', 'just', 'you know', 'I mean', 'very', 'anyway', 'sort of' and 'tend to' make up the rest of the Top Ten. These are all words or phrases which slightly obscure the meat of a line, the real intention – or gesture – behind it. Get rid of them.

The rest of the Top Twenty are all the phrases like 'haven't you', 'didn't I', 'shouldn't we', 'can't they' and so on, at the end of a line. Weed them out. Often they're a sign that you're not quite sure in your own mind of the progression from one line to the next. If actors put them in in performance, they're certainly a sign of uncertainty. Weeding them out makes you think about what the connection actually is. You may then find an alternative which expresses the intention and makes the connection more clearly.

In stage dialogue commas are the other main enemy. Basically a line of dialogue is a thought. A thought which has to be spoken. Spoken by an actor in one breath. Communicating a single thought. A thought which is important. (Geddit?) A sentence which rambles on with too many conditional phrases will diffuse its meaning – unless once again the effect is intentional. Look at every comma and see if it can be replaced by a full stop. If not, ask yourself how important the qualifying phrase is and, if it's doing nothing, weed it out. It will go for nothing on stage anyway. This is where reading your script aloud to yourself can be particularly useful, in order to discover at the very least where you've written a mouthful for the actors, whether it be sentences which are too long, unintentional alliteration or simply juxtaposed consonants which are difficult to say.

Check also for underlined words. They often work as red rags to a bull for actors (and these bulls are in your china shop); red rag because they signal that *something* should be emphasised. But the heat of performance and the personal syntax of different individuals being what they are, the actor may well emphasise the *wrong* thing and achieve the reverse of your intention.

Directions and false trails

A similar problem can occur with those little stage directions which you sometimes see at the beginning of a speech – 'Resignedly' or 'Hopefully' perhaps, or even 'Paling'. What these hopeful little directions mean in practice is hard to pin down. You may have a particular intonation in mind, but an actor may find his own better way of communicating the same intention.

The attempt to narrow a line down to one interpretation can back-fire badly, especially if an actor is so confused by it that it robs the line of all spontaneity. Better to rely on the context of meaning and the rhythm of the lines to suggest the way a line should be delivered than to depend on another person's interpretation of 'dejectedly'. Only when it's obvious that a line is so short and ambiguous that it could be read several different ways – 'I don't know' perhaps or simply 'Oh', and there is no alternative way of expressing that gesture consistent with the character – might these little adverbs make a useful appearance.

The same can be true of stage directions generally. Nothing demonstrates better the difference between real life and stage reality than directions like 'paling' or 'blushing' or 'a fat, bald man with two fingers missing', when a thin ten-fingered man with a healthy shock of hair is the best actor to present the force of the character. Detailed set descriptions, as implied when talking earlier about settings, can only limit the probably superior visual imaginations of directors and designers.

Similarly, attempts to suggest specific moves will fall foul of the actors' creative need to find their own best way to express your intention. Stage directions, from this point of view, are best regarded as a form of punctuation, indicating a flow and rhythm to the action, like rests in a musical score, rather than specific instructions. The simple indication 'Pause' is often more effective.

Dead wood

Many more scripts are overwritten than underwritten. Many I've come across, both in teaching and script-reading for theatres and other organisations, could be cut by a quarter. Sometimes, if you're writing for radio or television, you discover your script is grossly over length. Cutting it back ruthlessly can be an educational experience. Things come into much sharper relief through having to be shorter. Dead wood flies away. Try it as an exercise. Say to yourself 'This script has to be fifteen pages shorter' and be really savage with it. Chances are you'll see the improvement.

The great enemy of disciplined revision is resignation. Something may be almost right and, your will waning, you think to yourself 'That'll do'. A good way of facing up to the fact that it won't do – especially if, by now, your first draft is covered in scribbled corrections – is to write it all out again. The tedium of the task is such that the sheer effort of writing stuff again which repeats or wanders or delays getting to the point helps you to cut it. An advantage of working in longhand first is that much can be weeded out when typing. Word-processors are, I suspect, the enemy of economic dialogue.

Finally, when you've consulted your trusted guinea-pigs, converted their criticisms into action, made sure every line contributes vitally to the forward momentum of the action, weeded out your 20 per cent of repetitions, mannerisms and unnecessary directions to actors, you may just feel confident enough to pop the script in the post.

9
Into the market-place

The best excuse for delaying the rewriting of a script – apart from gaining distance from it – is the inordinate time it takes most theatres to consider it. If you've spent months reworking a script, there is nothing more irritating than waiting several more months to get a response, only for that response to suggest your first draft would have pleased them better. Almost every theatre will take months rather than weeks to consider a script. This is partly a result of the work involved in reading them, and occasionally a result of sheer indifference and neglect.

Most theatres receive dozens of scripts a year, if not hundreds, and no one can read more than half-a-dozen scripts a week without some kind of brain damage. Most people working in theatres already do more than just an eight-hour day. Script-reading is therefore fitted in around an already overloaded schedule.

Sometimes theatres have readers to whom scripts are sent out. Sometimes they have regular meetings at which people reading scripts exchange opinions. All of this involves further organisation. Occasionally – usually thanks to the various Arts Councils – a theatre will have a resident dramatist, a part of whose job is often to read or oversee the reading of scripts, and things may then move faster.

Whatever the system, it's sensible to build this delay into your own working timetable. If you're reasonably happy with a script, it may be as well to send it off and let someone consider while you're reworking. You will almost certainly have to rework again anyway before the play goes into production, and possibly again after that.

Against this, however, you should be aware that the odds against an unsolicited script's being produced are 100 to 1 or worse. A script needs not only to be well written but of particular interest and exceptional originality to be chosen for production. Many well-established writers have playscripts regularly turned down by theatres, so there is no shame in a large pile of rejection letters. Much of it comes down to offering the right 'product' at the right time to the right people. The answer is perhaps to rework *and* send off.

I think it was American playwright Edward Albee who said that an aspiring playwright's greatest asset was a large pile of carbon paper – this was before the days of cheaply available photocopying. And there is no doubt that the more scripts you have circulating to more theatres, the better your chance of success – until you reach that saturation point where they pick them up and say 'Oh no, not him again'.

Special agents

In case you're thinking 'They wouldn't think that if I had an agent', you should be aware that the same can come to be said about agents. The unfortunate truth is that there are too many scripts chasing too few production slots, and the chances of yours dropping into the right slot at the right time are worse than those of a roulette ball. It can be nearly as soul-destroying for an agent to send out scripts as for a writer and, though some agents will take new unproduced authors on – if they have distinctive talent – most, like everyone else in the business, are more interested once you've got a production.

This may seem like a 'Catch-22' but it makes sense for the writer too. An agent may give your script a slight edge over others, but most plays are produced through personal contact, and most first-time playwrights are produced in fringe theatres, of which there is now such a diversity that few agents can keep in touch with them all – even if they wanted to. There is, after all, no percentage – literally – in a play's playing to eight people a night on a profit-share basis. Agents therefore have little interest in, or influence over, the area of theatre most likely to produce a first play.

Some agents will respond to the special qualities in a script and work selflessly on its behalf, but this represents a personal commitment considered beyond the normal scope of their activities, and production is its ultimate goal anyway. That personal commitment is invaluable, particularly for writers who have no talent or taste for self-promotion. But is a close personal relationship with an agent worth more than one with a theatre? Personality and taste are considerable factors in these relationships, and it's possible that you would have more in common with the theatre people producing your play than with the agent. An agent can occasionally be an obstacle in that relationship.

The humdrum work of issuing and reading through contracts, negotiating fees and collecting royalties is the bottom-line function of most agents and is generally worth their ten per cent. But many agents also engage with the artistic interest of their job, and for them this is the more interesting part of it. Whether it's the sense of having participated in the discovery and promotion of a talent, the chance to influence the theatre we see, or the sheer fun of going places and being around the theatre world, an agent's view of your work will be conditioned by this side of his job.

This becomes important when he's advising you about work you've submitted to him, or giving advice generally about where to place plays and how to advance your career. It is obviously helpful if you share similar values and tastes. But in any case this will affect *your* view of his attitude to your work.

The range of agents is considerable. Some are specialists in film and television work, some have their best contacts in the West End, some are avid fans of the fringe, some are book as well as play agents, some seem more interested in work abroad than at home. The large agencies are the best known and have the most clout, but you're more likely to get swallowed up in them; the smallest can be very active on your behalf but their word carries no weight. Many writers' agencies make no written agreement with their authors and handle only that work which they are confident of placing. Very few theatre agents actively seek out writers' work.

You may desperately tout your work around them all before it's produced, and end up with one whose tastes you don't share and who offers you no further benefit. You can always change your agent later but, given that it takes a special commitment to try and place work for you, it could be better to wait till you have a production, when you may have a choice.

Available arenas

If you're being your own agent, where are the best places to send scripts? In London the Royal Shakespeare Company, the Royal National Theatre and the Royal Court all have script departments. The fact that they're organised in this way is a happy sign – in that you're more likely to get a considered reading and a fairly quick response. It's also a sign of the volume of scripts they receive and of being hived off as a separate department, at one remove from the directors.

This is important to bear in mind in any theatre. No matter how many people read and like a script, it won't be produced unless a director likes it and is encouraged to do it. Having a director who likes your work is often more useful than having a theatre. It's not until you put the two together that you have a production.

Outside the Big Three (who rarely produce scripts backed by outside directors), it's the smaller theatres who are most likely to respond to a new script, with or without a director in support. (Sometimes, of course, it can put a theatre off if a play comes pre-packaged with a director who isn't popular.) At the time of writing, theatres in London like the Bush, Hampstead Theatre Club and the Soho Theatre at the Cockpit have their script-reading well organised, usually with an actual literary manager, while theatres around London like the Tricycle, Stratford Theatre Royal, Croydon Warehouse, The Orange Tree at Richmond, the Lyric Hammersmith and Greenwich Theatre deserve special mention for commitment to new work when time and money permit.

Beside these, touring companies like Paines Plough, Out of Joint, Bubble Theatre, the Black Theatre Co-operative, Gay Sweatshop, Red Ladder, The Sphinx, Talawa and Tara Arts have shown a commitment to new work over the years – though some of these companies' policies have particular preferences, which it's best to find out about first. Children's companies like Polka, Pop-Up and Theatre Centre are also responsive to new work.

Outside London the Edinburgh Traverse, the Bolton Octagon, the Nuffield Theatre at Southampton and West Yorkshire Playhouse, along with the Royal Exchange, Contact and Library Theatres in Manchester, have been conspicuous in their support for new writing in recent years. Birmingham Rep, Nottingham Playhouse and the Wolsey at Ipswich also do new work when they can.

Beyond this there are small local companies, mostly out of London, who have received some funding for new work over the past few years, and I shall simply list them alphabetically. Action Transport, Altered States, Clean Break, Cleveland Theatre Company, Eastern Angles, Live Theatre, Major Road, Midnight Theatre Company, Northumberland Theatre Company, Plain Clothes Productions, Pentabus, Pilot Theatre, Profundis, Proper Job, Quondam, Raw Cotton, Remould, Rent-a-Role, Snap, Tamasha, Theatre Alibi and Vauxy.

A good way of finding out which agents and theatres to approach is to join a writers' organisation – anything from a local group to the national bodies like the Scottish Society of Playwrights, the Playwrights' Co-op, the Society of Authors, the New Playwrights' Trust, Theatre Writers' Union or Writers' Guild of Great Britain. The latter requires certain 'credits' for membership, but the TWU and the New Playwrights' Trust don't and have been the most useful to new playwrights in recent years.

The addresses and details of all the agents and companies mentioned above can be found in various directories, but the handiest is *Contacts*, published by Spotlight, who publish the actors' directory, 7 Leicester Place, London WC2H 7BP. But, with any theatre company, the most important thing is to have seen their work. That way you have at least some idea of its compatibility with yours. Seeing as much theatre as you can stomach is as good a way to learn your craft as meeting theatre people is to peddle it. In the end, hanging around in theatre bars may be as useful as free access to a photocopier.

Horses and stables

It is out of such contact with the life of the theatre that the desire to place a particular play with a particular theatre may come. You can, as it were, 'see' it going on there – and are perhaps loath to break faith with that feeling. This sense of identification with a particular theatre can be a wonderful thing, but it has to be reciprocated. If there is no obvious response from the theatre, there is no dishonour in sending scripts to more than one place.

Even for produced playwrights their relationship with producing theatres can be a very tenuous thing. Finer feelings rarely come into it. A playwright's agent may suggest sending a script to only one theatre because her business depends on keeping her good relations with that theatre sweet. Or she may resent the cost of further photocopying. The customary warmth and charm of theatre people can turn instantly icy cool when previously golden eggs turn bad and threaten to leave their substance all over the theatre's face. Playwrights themselves become desperate animals when erstwhile allies turn into apparent enemies – and, in a fit of pique, will send their scripts to the most unlikely people.

It's nice to think of playwrights being associated with particular theatres and, indeed, the most exciting work usually comes out of close and lasting collaboration between particular directors and writers. But the idea of stables of writers is largely based on mutual self-interest. There is something wonderful and heartening about the discovery of a new writing talent, but the constraints of 'the business' can soon turn this sense of belonging into a cynical exercise.

The idea of a writers' stable at certain theatres can be rooted in an extraordinary, proprietorial and paternalistic attitude which comes over theatre directors when they produce a new play successfully. The self-interest here, apart from simple pride or job satisfaction, is that, if the playwright becomes 'flavour of the month', the director's career suffers no harm at all. And since playwrights can go on to West End success and world renown, there can be considerable financial benefits.

Theatres also gain a lot of kudos with critics and arts-funding bodies for their promotion of new work. The small amounts of money paid to playwrights – for all my own and others' efforts in the writers' unions – are a small price to pay for this profile within the theatre community.

There are also benefits for the playwright in belonging: he has only to submit the script to one place, to people he knows and, so far, trusts – people who may indeed be shielding him from the severest critical judgement of his work. Whether this kind of paternalism is well judged is a moot point.

Inexperienced playwrights may well benefit from the hothouse treatment of insulated contact with a particular theatre's way of working – feedback, advice, attendance at rehearsals, etc. – while the delicate plant of their talent is nurtured. At the same time this can be symptomatic of a rather inward-looking attitude on the part of the theatre – a kind of cosy, 'we're-the-professionals' self-congratulation – which does nothing either to address itself to, or prepare the playwright for, the particular impact of their work in the world outside.

The impression of having arrived can be illusory for a playwright. Although a theatre may have first option on his subsequent plays, it can still reject them, and the truth is that with second or third plays it often does. Nothing is sadder than the sight of a playwright whose first play has been well received and who, thinking this is the break-through, gives up a steady job on the strength of that success, only to be brought down to earth by the rejection of his second play.

Such is the lack of real editorial insight around theatres that a script which doesn't work in first draft is rarely nursed along until it becomes producible. It's at this point that not the horse but the stable bolts. It can then be left to some hopeful young director to take the unwanted script up and either make his or her name, or a mess of it.

Directors and companies of actors who understand the writer's process and needs are unfortunately rare. The more they should be cherished therefore, and their opinion respected. Even then, however, it's unlikely that a genuinely good relationship will be soured if a script is shown elsewhere. The integrity of a good working relationship should be paramount but, if a company is slow to respond to a script for whatever reason, the writer has every justification in seeking a response elsewhere.

This can, of course, lead one into the parcel game which I described in my book on community theatre, *All Together Now*. Sending countless scripts to countless theatres can be a demoralising business. But not only writers are confronted with a largely postal relationship with theatres. Actors, directors and designers seeking and being offered work may well find that the only thing they have in common on the first day of rehearsals is the brown paper envelope they all clutch under their arms.

The peripatetic nature of most theatre work means that people can be brought together, from widely differing backgrounds and experience, to work together on a new play and find some common purpose within a very short period of time. On the whole the practice cannot be beneficial for new work, since the necessary tensions between strangers or those who have perhaps already encountered each other unfavourably – and even the tension between the two – serve largely as a distraction from the main business in hand. Nevertheless this practice remains the commonest in the theatre and should perhaps be experienced at least once by every playwright.

In general then it's as well to cast one's net wide, and there is no particular dishonour in sending scripts to more than one theatre at a time. Indeed, more than one playwright has benefited from sending scripts to two favoured theatres, informing both of the progress of the script within the other organisation, and thus raising the temperature of interest in his work. More recommended for experienced writers, this tactic can nevertheless work at even the lowlier level of readings and workshops. Such are the jealousies amongst companies competing for the crown of 'champion of new writing' that a first reading has currently acquired almost the status of a premiere.

A good one's hard to find

The one condition which should always outweigh this current emphasis on playing the market is a solid working relationship with either a director or a company. Taste in theatre is extremely subjective and, like good men, a good director is hard to find. As I remarked earlier, very few directors can actually read scripts, in the sense of responding to them as a conductor would to a musical score, simultaneously appreciating what's in them and how to bring it out.

Many directors, when it gets down to the rehearsal floor, are more concerned with their relationships with actors (with whom they're more likely to work again and therefore need), and some are even afraid of actors. Specifically, they are afraid that the fire which can spark between actors in the volatile process of rehearsal may be caught by a wind in the wrong direction.

In this sense directing is a very special skill and, though denigrating directors is a popular pastime amongst both actors and writers (and itself contributes to directors' paranoia), it should not be indulged in lightly. During production directing is as lonely and thankless a job as confronting the blank page.

The litmus test for directors, from the writer's point of view, is whether they approach a script with the attitude 'How can I do this play?' or 'What can I do with this play?' The latter approach betrays a lack of confidence either in the script or their own ability to make it live, and so they will be looking to extraneous devices – production effects or exciting but inappropriate performances from the actors – to save the play. If this is the case, it is already too late.

Much can be told from the way a director discusses a script prior to production. Either there is a genuine engagement with the themes and intentions of the play, accompanied by an emphasis on its best qualities and helpful suggestions for improvement, or there is a constant and demoralising harping on the play's problems, with reference only to how this or that will be difficult in production. Rarely do they offer a solution.

This is often the case with directors whose work before has been mainly on classical plays (whose authors are convieniently dead). Like actors with the same base of experience, they are used to working on texts which are immutable but can be cut to suit the circumstances. They are ignorant of the ways in which living authors work, and they handle badly the, for them, unusual situation of having one alongside them in rehearsal. They may believe that problems can be sorted out on the rehearsal floor. Unfortunately this doesn't work in the same way as for classical plays at all.

A living playwright in this situation has to be able both to remain in touch with his original intent and achieve an impersonal distance from it. The speed and immediacy of work on the rehearsal floor militates against this, but ultimately this is what a rehearsing company requires from a playwright. And it is rare that the immediate response of an actor to a script will illuminate a deeper-seated problem. There are no traditional ways of playing a new play, and all the professionalism in the world, tempered in the school of television and old plays whose qualities are well known, will not assist in the peculiar unravelling of the original and specific vision implicit in even the worst of new work.

Just a piece of paper

Many of the attitudes which militate against good working relationships between playwrights and theatre companies have been improved in the past decade, largely through the efforts of playwrights themselves. One way to anticipate the kind of ride you're in for is the contract issued by the producing company. Although a contract can never cover all the nuances of the subtle and complicated relations involved, it can be a considerable comfort in times of need.

The first rule with contracts is to make sure you have one. Events move quickly in the theatre world, and circumstances can change overnight. Some companies, particularly the smaller ones, are loath to spend valuable time on the boring detail of pseudo-legal jargon when the more exciting business of making shows is pressing. But the majority of enquiries I received during my time as a negotiator for the Theatre Writers' Union were from people who had no contract at all and suddenly found themselves caught out.

This was either because circumstances had changed and the company now wanted to do the show on different terms – making little difference to the company but a world of difference to the playwright; or the show had been successful beyond anybody's expectations, and now the company wanted to do one thing and the author another. Unless the understanding between writer and company is written down in black and white before production starts, there is no point at which the shifting sand of a production's progress can be held still, and those involved say 'That's what we agreed when we started'.

What's it worth?

In the mid 1970s the Theatre Writers' Union established the principle that a play is worth six months' pay at the company rate. This is in one sense arbitrary since a play can take two days or ten years to write. But it's roughly right if you look at the output of most full-time established writers, and it has helped to make the scales of payment for plays a little more realistic.

Subsequently it was also recognised that this must apply not only to commissioned plays but also to those which are already written and are then taken up, or optioned, by a company. Without this recognition playwrights would end up working to commission all the time; and the original play, written 'on spec', would disappear entirely. The consequences for the unique vision of writers, as opposed to hackwork, don't need to be spelled out.

The six-months principle is now enshrined in agreements for playwrights working with the Big Three and companies belonging to the Theatrical Managements' Association. There were several attempts to establish an agreement with the fringe companies before the current agreement with their umbrella body, the Independent Theatre Council (ITC), was established.

The realism of the six-months principle extends beyond merely feeding yourself while writing. Unless your idea is already well worked out, or the play is an adaptation of a book or play which already exists, a six-month writing period for commissioned plays is a better guarantee of doing your best work.

It may be acceptable while one is young and free of responsibilities to work quickly and 'get something on'. But, as one gets older and makes more demands on one's own work, thinking time becomes more and more important. For an unproduced playwright this may seem a distant prospect, but a considered play which earns respect within the theatre community and is perhaps produced over and over again is worth more than ten potboilers.

The six-month payments include royalties from the box-office takings of the first run of the play at a rate of between 7½ per cent (the minimum recommended by the Arts Council) and 10 per cent, the traditional percentage supported by the writers' unions. In some agreements this royalty is covered by a minimum guaranteed royalty, a form of payment originated by the Arts Council's former Royalty Supplement Guarantee (see later) to ensure that playwrights do not suffer financially through having plays performed in smaller auditoria at low ticket prices. Even with *ad hoc* companies there is usually the opportunity to apply for such a guarantee from the Arts Council – the success rate is better than fifty-fifty.

Protecting your baby

Perhaps the most important contractual conditions for the playwright lie beyond these purely financial considerations, in matters of what is called artistic control. These include the right to attend rehearsal at all times, the right to agree choice of director and cast with the management, and that no changes may be made in the text without the author's permission. Clauses which enshrine these principles, favourable for the playwright, are usually a sign that the company cares about the playwright's contribution and isn't uptight about his or her presence around the production.

A similar guide to a company's attitude towards a play can be detected in the way payments are staged. Besides the down payment for either a commission or an option, there is usually a delivery payment and/or acceptance payment. The gap between the two is slight but dangerously deep.

The first is literally what it says, a payment when the playwright completes the first draft of a commissioned play or delivers a rewrite of an optioned play to suit the particular circumstances of production (smaller cast and simpler set maybe, or shorter running time). This is simply a safeguard for the company that the playwright won't simply take all the money and run, and it should strictly be paid immediately upon delivery.

The acceptance fee is paid when the company is satisfied that they can go into production with the script: it is accepted for production. This is a perfectly reasonable clause if it means that the company recognises the playwright has done everything expected, everything within his power, to fulfil the original brief. It is not reasonable if it means the playwright doesn't get paid till every last foible and quirk of the director or acting company have been satisfied.

A good way to tell, besides the manner in which the clause is phrased, is to look at the payments. If the delivery payment is a mere token, or non-existent, and the acceptance payment is more than a quarter of the total, it means the company regards it not as a carrot to encourge the last drop of enthusiasm from a playwright but as a stick to beat him with, if necessary.

The final indicator of a company's attitude towards new work lies in what are variously called 'subsidiary', 'residual' or (presumptuously) 'participation' rights. These are payments, usually percentages of earnings, from the future life of a play if it is taken up and produced again, in the West End, on film or television, or by other companies.

The logic behind these 'residuals' is that a company makes a special contribution when it produces a new play (although companies are now claiming these rights as a matter of course) and should receive some reward if the play is successful. The presumption is that new plays represent of themselves a financial risk to theatres (though there is evidence to the contrary) and that the original producing management, for its courage in producing such a play, deserves to participate in its further financial success. Needless to say, there is no reciprocal clause recognising the contribution a play has made to a theatre's reputation. Neither is there a penalty clause for companies which make a mess of a play.

As this clause has become more and more common in writers' contracts, so the number of plays produced with an eye to further exploitation has increased over those simply done for their own sake. It is a pernicious clause not only for this reason, but for the assumption that the production of new work is not part and parcel of the life of the theatre. New plays are often glibly called 'the life's blood' of the theatre, but it is usually the author's which is extracted. My advice would be to strike such clauses out and agree to sign a further contract after production of the play if you do, indeed, feel the producing company deserves to be 'cut in'.

Subsidy for playwrights

I mentioned briefly above the Arts Council's Royalty Supplement Guarantee scheme which applied to most theatres not covered by writers' union agreements. Under this scheme a playwright received a supplement to the actual royalty earned which often enabled the playwright to write another play. Sadly this scheme has been discontinued.

There are other Arts Council Schemes, principally the Commissions and Options Awards for plays commissioned or optioned by theatre companies not in receipt of annual subsidy from the Arts Council. Under this scheme a company may receive a matching sum from the Council to complement whatever money they put up themselves when contracting a writer.

Arts Council bursaries are usually open only to writers with experience of stage writing who wish to embark on projects for which they're unlikely to be commissioned. The Arts Council also supports several residencies for dramatists with theatre companies.

Details of these grants and application forms are available in the Arts Council's annual brochure, *Theatre Writing Schemes*, available on request from the New Writing Officer, Drama, The Arts Council of England, 14 Great Peter Street, London SW1P 3NQ.

10
Into
production

Going into production with a play will bring home many of my comments earlier about the arena which, before you have a play produced, may well seem distant. Although it may all seem a bit abstract until you're working with actors, the pre-production period is vital. As stated before, you can learn a lot about your director in this period, and it's important to be involved in as many of the decisions as possible. This is not just to 'protect your baby' (though that can be crucial), but to bring the benefit of your longer-term acquaintance with the script to bear. This may sound an odd, almost impersonal, way to describe a writer's involvement in production, but I'm convinced it's most appropriate to the facts.

Just when you think your problems are over

The first thing to remember is that, however helplessly at everyone's mercy you may feel, to the others in the production you possess an enormous power. Your script has descended, godlike, upon them, rescuing them from unemployment and offering them a unique opportunity to shine. Few theatre people are aware of the extent of work behind a script. It appears instantly, and therefore seems to be instantly produced. They see only what's in front of them, so your months of toil are invisible.

What's more, it's *your* script they're working on, you're the reason they're all there, you're responsible for bits of their parts they don't like as well as the bits they do, they're all hell-bent on doing their best, and you should be grateful. You've had your say (the script is it), and now they're going to have theirs. The least you can do is show some humility.

Many of these attitudes are reactions to the parcel game and other aspects of theatre workers' employment and are purely psychological. Yet there is also some reality in them, if not truth, and it does no harm for the writer to lean back a little on the urgency of his own priorities.

In pre-production with a director, for example, it's important that you are present at discussions about everything – set, costumes, casting, publicity, music, choreography, touring schedules, the lot. Not because you need to *control* everything, but because you may be able to contribute an essential piece of information which others haven't yet noticed in the script, or which isn't in the forefront of minds mainly concerned with their own contribution to the production.

When discussing the set, casting and publicity in particular, the process of dialogue about the play between yourself, the director and others can represent an invaluable learning process about the play – for yourself as much as anyone. Not only do you get to see the play as others see it, but you can, as it were, define characters in real terms for yourself and the director, define the image of a play for the publicity person and define the look of the play for the designer. All this feeds back into your own knowledge of it and may set you off rewriting before anyone asks you to!

One voice

Any director who tries to exclude you from these discussions is either deeply insecure in his or her own ability, afraid of your power or afraid that you'll make an inopportune remark which will blur the lines of everyone's collective understanding about the production. Inexperience can mean that a writer goes directly for what he wants, rather than recognising the (sometimes roundabout) ways in which the individual skills of design and acting arrive at a result. This can obstruct an already established working relationship.

In a conventional production process, if the director says one thing, and the writer says, or even seems to say, another, it can lead to confusion. Everyone is taking a lead from the director, and one voice, his voice, should be paramount. A good writers' director will discuss with the writer beforehand or find a way of bringing the writer into discussion, so that his interests are upheld. Unless you're planning to take over the production – a ploy that's more often disastrous than successful – this is the situation to work for and accept. If it isn't happening, you can only try to suggest politely that it might be a good idea and hope that inexperience or ignorance has led to the lapse. If it's more than that, you're in trouble before you start.

Working with collectives

Some of the smaller fringe companies operate what is often called a 'collective' work method. This means that the director's power is not absolute, and usually that the company is in some sense led by actors. It may be that the director has been hired by the acting company, or that decisions within the company are made by the whole company, or part of it, together.

There have been successive waves of attempts to democratise the power of theatre directors over the years, and so the specific way in which this might work varies a great deal. Most directors, in any case, recognise that there is more to be gained from an acting performance which is ultimately liberated rather than fettered by direction. Where the ultimate power within a company lies with a group of actors, however, it can be confusing for a writer.

Any group of people who do the same job and work together develop a special understanding, and sometimes a special language, for the task in hand. They don't need to spell things out to each other, they 'know' what they mean. A writer working with a collective company of actors may not only not share that language, he possesses a power which can't be democratised beyond a certain point.

Unless a group of actors actually put pen to paper and shape the fabric of a script for themselves, the integral voice of a play remains that of the playwright. The best companies recognise this and allow the playwright as much space to practise his own craft as they demand in practising their own. Difficulties can occur, however, when a group of actors – or even a director – imagine that a writer is able, let alone willing, to realise on the basis of a rough outline their ideal play (or sometimes just their ideal role).

No amount of contractual fiddling can ensure that a playwright won't be asked to achieve the impossible, but once again much can be learned by reading between the lines of a contract. Principally, unless you are genuinely co-writing with others (they're putting pen to paper), the copyright in the play must always remain with the playwright. No amount of briefing by the company, no amount of improvisation or workshops to arrive at characters, no amount of criticism of the script and no amount of substituting alternative lines in rehearsal can truly be said to constitute writing.

All of the above contributes hugely to an actor's job satisfaction and usually decreases that of the writer. To ask for a cut of the royalties on top is sheer greed.

If things do go wrong, no amount of special pleading by the writer can make them right. Without the director's support you are placed in the invidious position of the 'difficult' writer: 'Not enough that you're responsible for all this and you're getting the benefit of our hard work, you make difficulties as well.'

To be there or not to be there

The shortness of most rehearsal periods means that there is a real pressure-cooker atmosphere in rehearsal where everyone has to get on with the job as quickly and efficiently as possible. All serious actors are in the profession because they too want to say something about life, but they say it literally through action, not endless discussion. Writers can come to be like hapless philosophers in rehearsal, spouting endless explanations that are no doubt true but not much use in the immediate situation.

A good director will set up the right time and place for a writer to make the general comments about the play which everyone needs to hear. But unless the writer has an exceptional working relationship with a director or a particular gift for working with actors, much of the rest of his time will be spent passively.

Without an active role in the proceedings, rehearsal can be very frustrating and, indeed, boring. Many writers prefer not to be around. But there will probably be five minutes in every hour when the director or an actor will need to know something, and only the writer can help. If you've been out of the room for fifty-five minutes, your answer to the question may seem to come from a different world. Either the director will need to translate your comment into the language that is already building up through work on the play or you may spend a quarter of an hour getting over the language barrier. Better perhaps to be bored for a while than to appear like an intruder from Mars at an inopportune moment.

So it helps if you're around at rehearsals – even if you're not there all the time. Chats with the director in the breaks, or daily on the telephone if you're away, can help to keep you in touch. Once again this should not be seen exclusively as a matter of *control*. A playwright – and everyone else – should look on his presence in rehearsal as assistance, not judgement. You shouldn't be a shadowy and rather sinister figure lurking in the stalls, but an active and contributing part of the process.

It may help to get to know the actors personally – in the breaks or after work in the pub – simply so that you get to know each other as people and build up a basis of trust and mutual understanding. The work on a play is always totally absorbing, and most people go on talking about it at every opportunity.

Taking part in this though, you need to be careful not to contradict anything the director has said in rehearsal itself. Unwittingly you could create confusion in people's minds or find your words manipulated by an actor to confront the director's authority. A good working practice will bear any amount of casual discussion but, where people are anxious or troubled, the playwright needs to tread carefully.

The old-fashioned, but unfortunately still extant, practice of asking a writer to leave rehearsal is often a product of an inability to reconcile traditional work methods with a writer's living presence. Most writers get bored and would sooner not be there all the time anyway. Occasionally writers can be difficult – either through inexperience or temperament, but they should always have the right to be there and to be informed of all decisions about the text in their absence. Usually they have lived with the play longer than everyone else in rehearsal put together, and it may be they know or can see something others can't.

Any 'difficulties' in the relationship should be worked through, as they would be with an actor, since the play will be just as much on show on the night as any actor's performance. But the reality is that the theatre has not reached the ideal stage where the writer's constant presence comes naturally, and for their part writers need to develop a sense of when, graciously, to retire. Far better that the writer has the confidence to let go of his baby than that he should be told.

This doesn't mean that you should be meek and retiring. At every stage in production, you should voice any disquiet you have – either discreetly to the director or, if asked in front of the whole company, to everyone. It may well make the penny drop for someone else if you do. But if your worry is met by an answer, however unsatisfactory, it may well be best to wait and see whether it's the worry or the answer which is justified.

At the very least you should allow people the space to find their own way to your script, even if that way is at variance with your own exact vision. Just as you should have the right not to change a comma unless you're persuaded it's in the best interest of the play, so you should respect a director's and actors' rights to develop the performances to the best of their ability. That way they're more likely to bring their own originality and energy into play, and you may be surprised at the gains, rather than losses, this brings. There can be an enormous generosity amongst theatre people, but it's rarely turned on tap by an ungenerous writer.

The instant scribe

Many companies view the opportunity of having the writer in rehearsal only as a way of getting the play rewritten. This may well be part of it, but most, and probably the best, rewriting is done outside the rehearsal room.

In the first place writers are accustomed to solitary work and to thinking about the play as a whole, backwards and forwards throughout its whole length, the consequences of one moment affecting another, one character affecting another. This takes time and can be seriously knocked off course by a sudden enthusiasm in rehearsal for a particular moment in a particular scene.

In the second place it is far better that actors' concentration in the usually short rehearsal span is not on what they're performing but on how to perform it. Confusion of the two can certainly be disastrous. (I have even known a line cut on the second day of rehearsal to reappear, ghostlike, on the third night.)

It's certainly a mistake if the director allows a kind of open house on the play where every individual's impression of the play (possibly week-old and once-off) is let loose on the script, and a wild mixture of contrasting viewpoints and prejudices is unleashed. If this happens, and the director does nothing to defend the script, he is either incompetent or wilfully attempting to undermine its authority.

Initial impressions can be useful, however, especially if writer and director have been so immersed in the script that a fresh eye reminds them of how an audience may see it first time. Knowing an actor's initial reaction to a script can also be important to the process of direction. It may even speed up the process by which an actor can find out how to play something. But there is no guarantee that this will turn out to be the right something. It may well lead to worse confusion, particularly *between* actors, later on.

In a tight rehearsal period, it is the writer's and director's responsibility to lead the acting company gently but clearly towards a collective understanding of what the whole play is about, so that everyone is freed to find their best way of interpreting their part in it. An actor who clearly understands the purposes of the play and is committed to them will render a play far more service than one who is confused and frustrated.

Only when everyone is familiar with the guts of the play (a good guide is when the time spent on it collectively by the company approaches that already spent by the writer) can all comment be considered equally valid. The real purpose of rewriting in rehearsal, given that writer and director have done their homework and got the script as near ready as their judgement can provide, is to free up particular performances, changes which a writer may well prefer to reverse in, for example, a published edition.

I once changed an actor's entire part. Not a particularly long part, it was nevertheless significant over a scene of about a dozen pages. The character was a foreigner whom I'd originally written in broken English but, discovering there was greater depth to him and a need for a subtler form of expression, I'd made his English only imperceptibly imperfect. The actor playing the part had difficulty getting a handle on the character and requested his English be more fractured. We sat down together and I rewrote the part back as it was originally, only for the actor to come back ten days later, having worked the character, and request that the draft as first presented be reinstated. He had, of course, needed to make the same journey with the character that I'd already been through, but simply explaining it was not enough.

Similar changes may be necessary because of the physical demands of production – a 'this' may become a 'that' because of the proximity of an object, a 'but' may become an 'and' because an actor's personal syntax means he can handle the thought process behind a line more readily that way. Sometimes the stage reality an actor has made of a part cries out for a rewritten speech or a differently timed entrance or exit.

That's how it works on the rehearsal floor, but go home and look at the script coolly, and you may well forget why it seemed a good idea in rehearsal. It will probably be the case that in another production that speech would remain as it is (and possibly another speech need adjustment instead). The point of the change in this instance – if your mind can respond to the actor's performance and, as it were, complement it – is to enhance the production, not the play.

There can unfortunately be another purpose behind demands for rewriting, and that is simply that an actor needs to feel important. For some actors it's a measure of their experience, wisdom and status that they suggest a line change and it's accepted. Actors themselves are usually better at detecting this motive than writers, in which case the whole company will soon want their lines changed – simply for the sake of it. This is, of course, nonsense and needs to be stopped as soon as detected, unless you are feeling indulgent and the change doesn't matter, or you owe the actor such a debt of gratitude you'll do anything for him. Sometimes you can only smile and shake your head.

It's a shame when status games of this or any other kind are played around the more pertinent business of discovering the play, because one can easily be mistaken for the other, leading to an atmosphere of mistrust. Otherwise there can be great pleasure in a sound rehearsal environment where trust abounds, and where the free association of the various skills creates a genuinely creative process.

But let no one believe that this is making the play. It is making the production. As stated before, it may well be that the playwright would prefer other productions to revert to the original version. It is a well-placed generosity towards the present production which allows this instant rewriting to occur. Hearts have been broken and mistaken claims on authors' royalties put forward because of a failure to differentiate between play and production.

One only has to compare the general suitability for further production of scripts forged in collective or workshop productions to see the difference, and how rarely the circumstances of one production apply to another. The more like a glove a part is made to fit a specific actor, the less likely it is to fit another.

Reviewing the reviewers

The life of a play after its initial production is, in the first instance, strongly affected by the response it gets, particularly from theatre reviewers. Good notices will mean bigger houses and the possibility of a transfer to a bigger theatre or the West End. A play performed by the Big Three or in the West End may well be published (though it's unlikely elsewhere).

'Success' in the theatre can be a very transient thing, however, and it's quite horrifying to look back and wonder what happened to plays and playwrights which seemed, only a decade ago, to 'say it all'. It's as well to bear this transience in mind when assimilating response, both good and bad, and from Joe Public as well as from reviewers.

Many newspaper critics revise their opinions on second viewing, and very few respond to individual plays as part of a playwright's whole opus. None of them will write about theatre as I remember a sports writer once reviewing a season of the cricketer Bob Willis's bowling. Everything was taken into account: the weather that summer, the state of the pitches, the complication of international and county commitments, team spirit, the effect of the introduction of the one-day game, his age, the problems of the fast bowler generally, even the problem of being Bob Willis. For some reason, even the most seasoned of theatre reviewers responds to only the product, never the process.

This limits the theatre's capacity to make advances, for process is more than half the key to doing it better next time. No amount of study of product alone will enable the generation of new work which extends the range of the theatre's potential. Comment on one's plays, friendly as well as hostile, needs to be related back to what went into them if it's to be of service in the future. A big success can ruin a playwright as easily as a huge flop. What matter most are the particular demands of your next idea.

Good luck.

11
Postscript:
the mind's eye

The evaluation of playwrights' work then, though a constant pastime (and not just for reviewers), is inevitably a matter of personal experience and taste. It's fun, and it offers a healthy stimulation of aesthetic criteria, but any cross-reference of good work from another playwright to one's own work is fraught with danger. One may respect and even learn from another writer's style, one may even aspire to achieve something similar; but just as the source of another person's work is different, so the final product of your own will be different. All playwrights regard their own work at the time of writing as supremely important, and quite right too.

For these reasons I've always tried to avoid value judgement when functioning as a teacher or literary manager. In the 'work-shop', when the editorial process is being carried out, the script in hand is the most important thing in the world, and everything else is a backdrop. In the first edition of this book I also resisted the temptation to raise one aesthetic approach above another, because a play can follow any style and work well, provided it remains true to the source of its inspiration. Nevertheless, the backdrop of stylistic choice is constantly present – I'm regularly asked about it in my classes – and indeed, the moment a play is out of the workshop and offered publicly, these questions become much more significant.

In particular, the question of realism versus other aesthetic approaches has come up more and more often in my class in the years since this book was first published. During that time the variety of artistic models on offer has increased even further, not least because of the growing interest in European culture following the changes in Eastern Europe. In the past we took much of our Anglo-Saxon dramatic tradition for granted, and what we broadly understand by realism is a big part of that. But what is regarded as great writing in one country may be seen as merely parochial in another.

Another time, another place

'What does an English actor act when he acts realism? What exactly is he acting?' This out-of-the-blue question was put to me as I left a week of writing workshops in Cracow. The question stayed in my mind for months, perhaps because it was like asking 'How do you breathe?' For a week British playwrights had been working with Polish playwrights, directors and dramaturgs, talking about our experience of developing new writing and taking as read something which for the Poles was not self-evident at all. Indeed, in any country where theatre has retained something of its mythical, ritualistic or visionary origins, the question would be just as pertinent.

Not only geography but also history play a part in developing taste. What one generation regards as the most pressing issue of its time, the next may find boring or irrelevant. Theatre is by its very nature of the moment, and fashion is a powerful conditioner of people's responses to it. The style of just one particular production can influence a whole generation. (Peter Brooke's *US* certainly influenced mine.) Luck also plays a part in popular success, as does the sheer determination of those who feel the world owes them a hearing. At the same time however, a play isn't just theatre; most plays can be produced a number of different ways, and many plays outlive the stylistic vogue of their first production.

None of this however addresses the way the fabric of a play is developed from perhaps an initially vague sense of its style (most often in reaction to a style it wishes to supersede) towards that original and unique 'voice' which the theatre constantly claims to be looking for. So maybe the time has come to look more closely at the implications of style. Not just what is intended by a particular approach, but what is actually achieved. I still believe you should find the best way of writing the play you want rather than the play someone (including yourself) thinks you *ought* to write, but there are some misconceptions about style and its consequences which are worth bearing in mind. What do you actually write when you write realism – and all the other -isms, come to that?

The real thing

In Britain we have a reflex towards realism, even when stylistically we imagine we want to get away from our predominantly verbal and psychological tradition. I have talked a little about this in Chapter 6, but there are some further considerations, deeply central to the question of style, which need to be acknowledged. First, the difference between naturalism and realism (for they are often used indiscriminately to mean the same thing, and this only leads to confusion). 'Naturalism' in my mind refers strictly to turn-of-the century, mainly European, literature, whose principle aim was to portray to its public the actual living conditions of poor and working-class people, in the belief that this could induce social change. 'Realism' is defined traditionally still as reflecting the contemporary real world, but through the essence rather than the detail of particular characters and events.

The distinction is important even if only to define what it is that many people find unsatisfying about television drama. Also because, from my very first weeks in professional theatre to the present day, it has been the prerogative of the young to rail against 'naturalism' and/or 'realism', while the forms they have put in its place have themselves been confusingly varied. So many of my writing students over the years have declared that they are trying to do 'something different', while their actual writing has been powerfully determined by one kind of realism or another.

Another misunderstanding can also be at work here, namely the belief that a 'theatrical' style of production can transform an otherwise conventionally written script. Words like 'stylised' or 'heightened' are commonly used to describe the imagined effect; latterly, the word 'expressionism' has been hijacked for this purpose (again with scant awareness of its historical definition), and the colloquial use of 'surreal' is also eroding its specific connection to the dream-like unconscious in art.

All of these abuses point nevertheless to a widespread desire to get away from the mundane reflections of real life we see in television drama, most notoriously in the 'soaps'. This desire is important, not least because it reflects the unique potential of live theatre to transcend mere mimicry. At the same time, one cannot ignore the interdependence of theatre on television and film. The industries are closely connected, and acting skills have been profoundly influenced by televison. Yet while television helped to make both film and theatre 'realer' until the 1970s, theatre has reciprocated with non-realist approaches since the 1960s which have subsequently transferred to film (notably in the 1980s), and have now even come into television. The vogue for comic-strip images in brassy colours, whether in futuristic or film-noirish subjects, is just one example. However, the realism of the camera (or perhaps one should say its literal-mindedness, as described in Chapter 5) remains a point of genuine difference. As do the technical limitations of the stage.

For example the film of *Batman* attempted to evoke the fantastical world of Gotham City by non-realistic means with carefully constructed sets, and even artifically stretched Jack Nicholson's mouth as The Joker. All this added up to, however, was a painstaking recreation of the comic strip. When they put the story in front of the camera, they made it as close to the 'real life' of the original as possible. What's more, much of the acting (apart from Nicholson) was in the laconic, tongue-in-cheek, tough-guy style associated with hundreds of American movies. Because the camera supposedly doesn't lie, what you put in front of it is hard pressed to be a metaphor. By comparison, stage acting is automatically artificial; the actors all face the same way and speak unnaturally loud. If to this given artificiality you add coloured light, long shadow and distorted building shapes, it is like a tautology. The stage cannot help but be a metaphor.

Nevertheless, audiences watching both forms will be making connections with their own experience. I say 'experience' rather than life, because reading *Batman* comics is hardly living. Similarly an audience I witnessed watching a Polish production of Brian Friel's *Dancing at Lughnasa* followed its evocation of Irish rural life with a fascinated if distanced curiosity, but became really engaged when the question arose of whether the devil was inspiring the dancers. In other words it is a matter of what an audience wishes or is able to see as much as what is intentionally shown.

In Britain we're used to the idea that even the most colourful, physical and effect-laden productions, full of dance, exaggerated movement and song, are invariably trying to say something about present-day life. Could it indeed be otherwise? Well it might. In Europe for example, many plays and productions relate directly to the life of the mind, to the world of ideas. But surely, you might think, a play which analyses present-day social behaviour through, say, mime, is a play of ideas? Not really. Not alongside a play in which, for example, the behaviour of the characters demonstrates the difference between the belief in God and the belief in religion. In other words, not a play whose ultimate purpose is to show (by whatever means) something about life itself, but to point (even through the most conventional staging) to something about the way we *think*. The ultimate question addressed is not present-day living but a tradition of thought.

This may seem a fine distinction, but it is crucial to a proper understanding of non-realistic drama, and to the import of its styles into British theatre. Too often, because we can't understand the language of Polish or German or Japanese theatre, we've responded to its visual style in isolation. Thus 'Brechtian' comes to mean bare stages with lots of hessian and songs. What we forget is how theatre in other countries occupies a different place in the intellectual and cultural traditions of those countries, how indeed the perception of what an action on stage finally comes to *mean* is conditioned by those traditions.

Meaning is the ultimate point of a theatrical presentation. It matters that an audience receives something from a work of what it's intended to transmit. English audiences however are so attuned to watching the interplay of social manners, they are often blind to comment on the way we think. Those British plays which do primarily address the life of the mind (prejudice, say, or lack of self-awareness) are often sold short because recognition of social manners – the means to convey the idea – outweighs recognition of the idea itself. This is not an argument in favour of abstraction or over-seriousness, but an observation about the limitation of our expectations as audiences, and the 'realism' which so strongly conditions them.

Talk to any foreigner about a performance you've just witnessed together, and it will soon appear that you were watching a different play. Come to that, talk long enough to someone from a different background or generation, and you may experience the same feeling. What goes on in the head of audiences is unpredictable and often astonishing, and this is indeed one of the great joys of performance. But in the end meanings are being constructed, whether they conform exactly to those intended or not. Everything has some sort of meaning. Die-hard opponents of seriousness and abstraction are simply lining up in favour of frivolous and self-evident meaning.

Technical switch

This has consequences when one considers technical innovation. How, for example, do you show a horse on stage? A pantomime horse is an almost immediate invitation to laugh. The spectacle of two human beings contorted to represent an animal is funny. But it's also funny when you have a real horse on stage and it shits. Even if special effects men were able to produce a mechanical horse, lifelike in every detail but programmed to behave itself, like as not the audience's attention would be more absorbed by its technical perfection than its true meaning within the story. Its technical perfection might even come to seem rather sinister. It would be difficult therefore to tell a realistic story on stage about or involving a horse without running into the technical limitations of the stage as a medium. On the other hand to see what is obviously an actor play an animal and *interpret* its familiar physical characteristics can be a fascinating stage event. The very acknowledgement (*pace* Brecht) that this is stage reality liberates the imagination in a way that slavish attention to naturalistic detail cannot. By contrast, the same performance on film might well look stagey; yet we have no problem with the mechanical monsters of *Jurassic Park*.

The other obvious technical features which create meaning are lighting and sound. Theatre fashion over the past two decades has seen a switch from neutral white light for everything to powerfully atmospheric and suggestive lighting and even the stage equivalent of film soundtracks. Tilted stages, unlikely staircases and trapdoors have all made a comeback. What is interesting about this fascination with the toy theatre's box of tricks is that we don't *believe* in the spectacle (as the Victorians did), nor do we see them as a kind of refracted inner reality (as the Expressionists did). We see them for what they are: technical effects. In other words our view of what we see on stage has become more 'naturalistic' (or literal-minded), while the technical means have become more fantastical.

I've used the word 'technical' deliberately to describe these various components of stage illusion because it's easier to think about them that way than dialogue. Yet dialogue is also part of the stage reality, and our view of it is affected by the same influences as our view of set, lights and costume. On one hand we follow where dialogue takes us, absorbing its meaning. On the other, we are also detached from it, seeing it for example in the revival of a play from the 1960s as perhaps 'dated' or 'mannered'. We could equally well make the same criticisms of a restoration comedy, but we wouldn't. We don't expect its language to reflect modern reality. When exactly the same criticism is made of a play like John Arden's *Serjeant Musgrave's Dance* which consciously uses stylised dialogue, you begin to wonder whether such criteria are at all appropriate. My own play *Female Transport* has been criticised for the exact opposite sin – using contemporary language in an historical setting. Yet in both cases the choice is as deliberate as the choice of cardboard props by a designer; it is technical.

I've spoken elsewhere (Chapter 5) of the overwhelming influence of television and film on aspiring playwrights' dramatic vocabulary. To the influence of 'TV naturalism' as seen in the soaps, sit-coms and those 'heritage' series which play on nostalgic clichés of England's self-mythologised past (whether flannelled fools or repressed Victorian sexuality), must now be added the largely visual impact of TV advertising: swiftly cut images, affective lighting and 'de-naturalised' shooting, whether by unusual angles on real subjects, or straightforward synthetic images.

All this has added a richness to the vocabulary of the imagination, though not always a consistency in the face of sustained narrative.

There has been much deploring of the short attention span induced in today's younger generation by swiftly crosscut television. But this is only a problem when the interest of a drama *requires* a more lingering, deeper appreciation of its characters and situations. A visual image may be powerful for three seconds and may indeed do the work of ten minutes of dialogue, but it can also be incongruous when juxtaposed with the techniques of more sustained story-telling. Where the purpose of the play is to draw us into the lives of the characters, an audience will need time for this interest to register. It is as though a natural timespan of assimilation is necessary for certain qualities in a story to sink in (and the precise timing of this can often rest finally with the actor's performance). Too short and the play becomes a comic-strip, too long and it becomes pedestrian and obvious. It was interesting to observe, for example, how the rhythm of the Monty Python team's sketches, successful over a few minutes, failed to sustain interest when the team attempted its first feature films. Like the pantomime horse, the technique of the three-second image can be difficult to assimilate into the overall meaning of a couple of hours.

Past the postmodern

But if it's also a matter of what an audience *wishes* to see, one has to acknowledge that public awareness has also grown. Each individual's personal log of watching hours is expanding constantly. Children grow up watching television; students study hours of videos and old movies; professional commentators can spend all day watching something or the other. When we see an actor with a telescopic rifle and his back to us, we instantly read 'unknown assassin'. (Compare this, incidentally, to 'primitive' peoples who, never having seen film before, look *behind* the screen for its reality.) With these familiar shorthands, stories can be told with great speed.

Alongside this expansion of our visual sophistication everything involving dialogue – from length of characters' speeches, through length of scenes, to the length of plays themselves – has been curtailed. Visual information has been recognised as being faster and more directly digested than verbal information. On one hand, it may seem that dialogue itself has been devalued. On the other hand, the function which dialogue performs has become more acute. What has really happened is that a certain kind of perception has become quicker. Some might say it has also become more superficial. But the great strength of television as a medium is that it broadens outlook. To require that it also deepen 'inlook' is perhaps asking it to look two ways at once. The significant point is that film and television as media have altered perception, and therefore altered meaning.

And as further generations grow up having watched television from childhood, not only the distanced sophistication described above but also the postmodern phenomenon of comment upon previous artworks will no doubt become part and parcel of the interest in new work. In this context a greater onus is placed on story-tellers to avoid cliché and remain original. Stalked by the shadow that there are no original stories left, they step gingerly from original moment to original moment as if through quicksand unless, like a David Lynch, they use cliché self-consciously as a kind of comment.

In Eastern Europe they have been picking their way across quick-sand of another kind for decades. The Polish 'Theatre of Allusion' sums up the response of artists there to a dramatic vocabulary limited by censorship. Unable to tackle real-life issues head-on, artists resorted to parallel situations (whether in history, fiction or fantasy) to allude to their real subject. Audiences also became adept at reading the allusions, only feeling they could 'read' the story once they'd twigged its reference points. Meanwhile, in the West, audiences have to keep on their toes to understand references to situations from old movies, even 'quotes' of particular shots (like when a jazz musician inserts a phrase from a well-known tune into an improvisation).

Looking lively

All this indicates how active the mind is when we watch drama. The sophistication born of increased familiarity with all kinds of dramatic media has simply heightened our ability to recognise, and therefore pigeon-hole, style. It's easier to build a common consensus of appreciation around familiar experience than to forge ahead with new experiments with the medium's uniqueness. Drama will always offer a mixture of new insights built on old perceptions; the question is what kind of notation is appropriate to making a new tune live on an old instrument?

For live theatre remains primarily a flesh-and-blood experience. For more than twenty years people have argued that the decline in live theatre audiences is compensated by the uniqueness of the experience offered. Yet the effect of the past decade's economic stricture upon theatre in Britain has been to revert (and not always self-consciously) to styles and manners associated with the theatre of the 50s. But for a dramatist with something distinctive to say about our times, striking the appropriate stylistic balance between familiarity and innovation is crucial. Not only that, but what is suggested to the mind by witnessing actors' work is, one hopes, complemented by what is demonstrated to the senses. 'God, you're beautiful when you're angry' is recognised as a cliché in dialogue, but we can still watch the actual performance of desire grow in one character as anger grows in another with fascination. We can also (just about) accept the line said with self-conscious irony. In both cases, to see this action performed live is to re-examine its present-day relevance close to. With this in mind, stage dramatists need to be aware not just of the climate of ideas around a play, but of how its physical and sensual experience will communicate.

What then actually happens when a play is performed before an audience? The truth of the matter, and its excitement, is that few, if any, assumptions can be made with certainty about how an audience will react. The most extreme example I encountered of this was during a staged reading of my play *Free Time* to a Polish audience during those writers' workshops in Cracow. I chose the play because it is about the relationship of self-styled socialist intellectuals to the political realities of a writers' conference during the Spanish Civil War. The Polish actors, customarily used to several months of rehearsal, flung themselves bravely into the reading with next to no preparation but total commitment, and the first half went so well that two agents approached me in the interval, and a television crew arrived to film the second half.

Needless to say, the crew's presence subsequently proved to be a distraction to the actors, but something else dampened the excitement. A character called SIS has a speech at what turned out to be a crucial point in the second half. I had not realised how crucial. SIS is typical of a certain breed of 1930s middle-class, English communist. A brusque, down-to-earth and efficient organiser, she is also like a mother to the delegates. She has a warm, human streak, which she plays down, and one can only imagine her dressed in English tweeds and woollens with very sensible shoes. The actress playing her in Poland, who clearly relished the part and played it with considerable insight, nevertheless had the tough, hard look which we in the West have come to associate with communist women in positions of power.

And so did the Poles. When the speech was delivered – it is about how style and the herd instinct can as easily become a substitute for clear thinking among radicals as anyone else – it meant something quite different to the Polish audience. It meant blood and imprisonment, whereas for a British audience it might've meant yuppies and the Poll Tax. Although the play was set in the 1930s, when Stalinism was barely a concept, and the characters were English, the appearance of the actress and the difference in situation of the audience turned the meaning of this speech into something else. Needless to say the audience afterwards were quick to point out that when an Englishman talked about socialism it meant something rather different to a Pole.

Horses for courses

That is an extreme example, but something similar goes on in every performance of a play. Even from one night to the next, the composition of the audience in terms of age, class, nationality and gender, will vary. A 70-year-old butcher from Inverness will see a play differently from a 22-year-old waitress from Hitchin. Not only that, but the mood people are in affects the way they receive a play. Furthermore, but the way one person receives a play affects the way the next person receives it, and so on.

None of these observations is new, but there are consequences of these theatrical facts of life which often go unconsidered. If a seminal French play of the 1920s can only be played successfully to English audiences like Noel Coward, what chance the uniqueness of a new play? If an actor who has played Inverness and Hitchin many times has worked out a delivery which, though not guaranteed to 'succeed' (which in England usually means get a laugh) every time, will work on most occasions, why subject oneself to the uncertainties of unknown territory? Such a guaranteed delivery may not, however, be consistent with the underlying themes of the play. Get enough of these 'experienced' wrinkles, and they may even accumulate to the point where they destroy the impact of the play entirely. Furthermore, a style of playing built up on this 'experience' can begin to act as a model for what people write. In the end the uniqueness of each play disappears under the accumulation of stylistic accretions to the point where each performance becomes nothing more than a celebration of a particular kind of theatre-going habit. ('We go because you can always count on good-value entertainment'.)

This is so different from the European experience where, although bound by its own limitations, actors and audience alike are on the lookout for what the work *means*; where actors may well refuse to commit to an interpretation of a part until they have some sense of how the play will be interpreted as a whole. Meaning in this sense is not just what you put into a part, but what will be taken out of it by the audience; not just a matter of the physical phenomenon on stage which everyone witnesses together, but of *what is made of it*, how it will connect with ideas and opinions which are current amongst the audience at the time.

After all, the audience cannot act the play with the actors, they cannot share directly the experience of feeling the character, they are necessarily *outside* the actor's work, looking on. The real communication of a play is therefore, is not what is felt by its actors, not even what they transmit as performers, but what is received.

These things are often forgotten, particularly when developing an aesthetic theory of theatre. Usually, aesthetic theory concerns itself with intent – what a performance is hoping to achieve – rather than its actual effect. There can be a huge gap between the two, and nowhere is this more noticeable than when one steps outside the cosy world of one's own dramatic heritage. Perform in a working men's club or anywhere abroad, and glib assumptions about *exactly what* is being communicated lie in smithereens.

Indeed, the more thoroughly experimental and unfamiliar a play, the more surprising an audience's interpretation can be of a particular gesture or phrase. If an audience is completely disorientated, a quizzical smile can become a sadistic grin, a raised eyebrow can become a threat. It may be the wrong impression, but it is a real one. And the same miscommunication can occur within any style of theatre, realistic or otherwise. Whatever their expectations beforehand, audiences become locked into an understood context for the playing out of human will in conflict. Sometimes that conflict is emotional, sometimes intellectual, but it is always interpreted through its physical signals. In Britain we lay emphasis on whether those signals correspond to our idea of real life. We also respect emotional honesty in our actors relating this to real-life feelings. But the same honesty is looked for in other cultures, where the emphasis may be on the life of the mind, only here it may be called 'consistency of interpretation'.

In many respects the same thing is acted whether you act realism or expressionism or absurdism. The range of expression available to the human body is, after all, finite. Extending one faculty – movement or dance, for example – will tend to reduce its range for speech. Conversely, the more intricate and subtle the dialogue, the less opportunity there is for physical expression. The biggest difference lies not in what occurs in the arena itself (see Chapter 2), but within the audience's mind.

Moreover, a production's aims can get through to an audience even if they are imperfectly realised. The merest glimpse of a different artistic approach, because it heralds a new thought or idea, can be more satisfying than a well-oiled, conventional production.

Part of the appeal of theatre for a certain section of the audience will be precisely that something is on offer which cannot be seen elsewhere. Indeed, the 'exotic' appeal of theatre increases the more widespread and institutional dramatic entertainment becomes in cinema and TV. The glimpse of some vision beyond the mundane and familiar will always remain central to the attraction of live theatre.

Realising the impossible

All the sadder then that an actor's 'experience' can reduce the unique vision of a play to an over-familiar cliché. Theatre remains one of the most conservative art forms precisely because so many people, with all their various understandings based on previous experience, are involved in its production. Each new dramatic idea is subjected within its system of production to a levelling form of Chinese Whispers.

In recent years this levelling process has been complicated by the increasing movement of actors between stage, film and TV. Not only does this have the obvious effect of encouraging television acting on stage, but the way film and TV are shot – according to the dictates of finding locations rather than the unfolding of a story – and the way theatre rehearsal schedules are affected by actors' film and TV commitments, have shifted the emphasis of dramatic writing away from sustained narrative and consistent characterisation to the power of 'the moment'. An actor who has received that rare form of feedback, unqualified praise, for a particular moment in a TV performance could be forgiven for believing such an approach is the key to success on stage. But if this 'experience' is brought into the rehearsal room, it may be inappropriate. You cannot hold a moment until the director shouts 'cut' on stage. You have to get out of it into the next moment, and the next, and so on.

The very fact of live theatre's being a continuous form (along with its necessary timespan for assimilation) can create problems for experimental work based in an appreciation of visual 'moments'. As an audience you can find yourself watching the progress of a physical narrative, culminating in a particular moment or 'tableau'; then suddenly the needs of the narrative change, the illusion is broken, and instead of continuing its narrative momentum, we simply watch the actors troop off stage. Something similar can happen with writing influenced by television: a scene ends in a powerful 'moment' with several characters on stage, and the next scene starts in a different location with a different set of characters; on television you just cut to the next scene; the assumption is that on stage you have a blackout, and the equivalent effect is achieved.

But not only is it more difficult to time the blackout live, you effectively halt the forward momentum of the story for a few seconds while actors stumble on and off and sets are moved. Both these forms of theatre, one highly physical, the other highly 'naturalistic' fail to recognise the overriding importance in live theatre of continuity of narrative, the stringing together of one moment to the next.

To sum up then, the process of 'realising' a script, or even an idea, is necessarily subjected to not only the cultural but also the technical traditions within which it is being performed. Whether in television or stage, these traditions in Britain are predominantly realist. Thus, partly through linguistic limitation or accident, there is a double pressure towards the representation of real life. You are 'realising' realism. At the same time it is important to recognise the difference between making a performance live (which it can do without being at all realistic) and attempting to represent real life.

This can lead to confusion, both for the dramatist and for the audience. It is perhaps no surprise that directors, both in film and theatre, have embraced the new visual vocabularies of film and TV with greater alacrity than playwrights. The director's responsibility is to expose the story from moment-to-moment, whereas the playwright's is to string those moments together. For both director and writer, however, the ultimate task is to understand the momentum behind each moment, to find, if you like, the connecting tissue. Instead of each image representing only a frozen moment in time, to find what makes the story move on from frame to frame, from beat to beat.

Stringing pearls

What we associate in our minds from what we see enacted physically before us is therefore an important part of the action in any dramatic representation. Moments are linked not just by story but by association. The connecting tissue is allusive (like the theatre in Poland) as well as emotive.

Is there any generalised way in which we can understand this further complication on the theme of intention and effect which I described in Chapter 8? And can we put that technical understanding to creative use in our writing?

For the playwright the most crucial technical tool is language. How many productions has one seen which are boldly announced as 'expressionist' or 'surreal', in which the stage is bathed in purple light, the characters walk on stilts, wear masks, juggle and grunt to background music, but the moment they put sentences together they are of the order of 'I don't feel very well today' or 'Did you enjoy your dinner?'

The point is that getting away from naturalism doesn't lie primarily in theatrical effect or visual imagery; it lies in what one might call the synapses between lines of dialogue, the connection between one line and the next, and whether the actors and audience are being asked to make a connection beyond the merely mundane. If you take just a few lines from Pinter or Beckett, you see very quickly how the differentness of their worlds is established.

JERRY: How's it going? The Gallery?

EMMA: How d'you think it's going?

JERRY: Well. Very well, I would say.

EMMA: I'm glad you think so. Well it is, actually. I enjoy it.

JERRY: Funny lot, painters, aren't they?

EMMA: They're not at all funny.

JERRY: Aren't they? What a pity. (Pause) How's Robert?

EMMA: When did you last see him?

JERRY: I haven't seen him for months. Don't know why. Why?
EMMA: Why what?

JERRY: Why did you ask when I last saw him?

EMMA: I just wondered. How's Sam?

JERRY: You mean Judith.

EMMA: Do I?

JERRY: You remember the form. I ask about your husband, you ask about my wife.

EMMA: Yes, of course. How is your wife?

JERRY: All right.

VLADIMIR: Where was I. . . How's your foot?

ESTRAGON: Swelling visibly.

VLADIMIR: Ah yes, the two thieves. Do you remember the story?
ESTRAGON: No.

VLADIMIR: Shall I tell it to you?

ESTRAGON: No.

VLADIMIR: It'll pass the time. (Pause) Two thieves, crucified at the same time as our Saviour. One –

ESTRAGON: Our what?

VLADIMIR: Our Saviour. Two thieves. One is supposed to have been saved and the other. . . (he searches for the contrary saved). . . damned.

ESTRAGON: Saved from what?

VLADIMIR: Hell.

ESTRAGON: I'm going. (He does not move)

This uniqueness, the sense of a stage reality being established through what is unspoken but understood between the lines is quite different from a direct attempt to reflect real conversation. Pinter's lines in isolation may echo the quirkiness of real London speech, but their connecting thread is a unique kind of agnosticism. Similarly, Beckett's characters, behind their deceptively everyday concerns, constantly confront a dreadful void. Both offer a patina of familiarity, but the uniqueness of both lies in what remains unsaid.

In fact these unspoken understandings are in every writer's work (though not always used so effectively). As with the passive nervous system (those reflexes like breathing and feeling pain which the body performs automatically without the conscious control of the brain), they lie constantly just below the surface. How many times have I observed in rehearsal of my own or other writers' work actors struggle to make conscious a meaning which is opaque to them but so crystal clear to the writer he can't even explain it adequately. ('How do you breathe?' 'Like this.' 'No, but how do you do it?' 'The way I always do.') The most personally felt, and therefore most original, part of our writing is often that which is least conscious. It is as though there were a torrent rushing through an underground cavern, and every so often a line or two splashes up through a crack to the surface. If you follow the line of splashes along the ground, you may begin to see where the underground torrent leads.

As observed in Chapter 5, each of us has our own personal syntax, conditioned broadly in the first instance by geography, generation, class and education; but then crucially by personal experience, including our experience of drama. This means that each word or phrase we use has a set of special connections for us as individuals, and it is through these connections that we build the unique world of our plays. Realising that a passage of dialogue is tapping into a special, even if unarticulated, zone of tension is one of the great aesthetic pleasures of writing, both for its author and for subsequent readers. It is also through discovering those connections and tensions for themselves that directors and actors can begin to inhabit that world.

Proving the pudding

Once a script is taken up by an actor, the correlation between the experience expressed and its playing out is acutely tested. Does the way the playwright has notated this experience make the desired connections? It is not until the playwright's words are, as it were, plugged back into physical life that their bearing on our shared experience of those connections can be tested. For this reason I am critical of those writers who believe good actors can take up any old script and make it come alive (they can but that's not the point). I am also critical of those actors who seek to rewrite dialogue to make it fit their performance. Indeed, if I read another *Radio Times* interview with a film star used to rewriting their parts, then encounter a young actor straight out of drama school hoping to do the same on a stage play, I shall sue everyone involved.

The whole point of the interplay between the two skills is the stretch between them. A playwright juggling several characters at a time can miss a particular connection of a character's words, and so can an actor. Streamlining dialogue to fit one particular character's 'through-line' can seriously impoverish the tension and richness of the play overall and thus, incidentally, the actor's performance as well. What is important is that neither skill ignores the all-important dialectic (also discussed in Chapter 5) between being inside a character and feeling it, while retaining a subliminal awareness of how it looks from outside.

The closer the language of our plays reflects the concerns of the present day, the easier it will be for interpreters and audiences of our work to plug into what we have to say. Language is not an accident; it is the pragmatic means through which the human species enables itself to get on with its important business. It may not always be accurate, but it attempts, by definition, to be effective. Those words and phrases which aren't effective get discarded. Because of this, language is always changing. Phrases fall in and out of fashion according to the priorities of a particular age. Because of this, we can only write in the language of the present day. Any attempt at pseudo-historical speech, at a 'heightened' style which (like the strictures of the Académie Française) attempts to impose an unnatural ambition upon that underground torrent, or at a revived poetic style which doesn't address the accumulated reasons for preferring 'realistic' dialogue, will be sloughed off like a rejected skin graft.

Even when we find a successful 'stage language', it is inevitably rooted in the language of the time of its writing, just as the experiences which has prompted it and to which it refers, are also of its own time. At some level then, the only direct experience of a play is in the meaning its language conveys at the time of its writing. So not only language, but the emotions and thoughts of the characters and their situations, and the overall view we have of them is rooted in their time. In this sense, the more a writer is attuned to immediate and contemporary uses and meanings of language, the more vivid its performance by actors will be and the deeper its appreciation by audiences.

This seems like a very strong argument in favour of realism. Yet strictly it only addresses means, the 'realising' of an end rather than the end itself. If a play were addressing the difference between belief in God and belief in religion, it might have to show God as a character, and who knows how God speaks (other than in mysterious ways)? My point here is that whether a play is written in 'realistic' language is conditioned in the first instance by its subject-matter, but that ultimately the author's being in intuitive touch with his own underground torrent and communicating it to a present-day audience will shape its particular form of expression.

If you're lucky enough to have a play produced several times by different companies over a number of years, you also begin to see the difference between what is immediately suggested by the language of a scene, and what remains of its central essence. Writers always hope that their plays, first time out, will be cast optimally – that is, with the very best actors whose stage presence most closely fits the qualities of their characters. But if you move outside those expectations – to a production in a foreign country, an amateur production, or even a youth theatre production – you begin to see something beyond the literal depiction of a person. The actors involved cannot hope to present the play as originally intended, but they inevitably attempt to portray what is suggested by it. The veneer of immediate realism is stripped away, and the purely dramatic ingredients of plot, narrative and situation play a stronger part in determining what actually happens on stage. You see the force behind the character, rather than its verbal or social trappings.

A similar effect can be observed in playreadings as a means of trying out scripts. A well-cast, well-executed reading can obscure faults in a play which a badly performed reading will reveal. One can also see something similar happen now with plays written in the 1960s or 1970s, where what we think of as 'dated' language is like a cobwebby shroud hanging over the subtext, in itself rather vital, going on underneath. On one hand, it makes one wonder what the contemporary response to Shakespeare's language could have been; on the other, it reinforces the suspicion that four hundred years of unrelenting progress towards 'real' dialogue has distracted us from the real issue.

A book like this is not the place to recommend one style of theatre above another. One can safely say, however, that the wholesale importation of a particular visual or technical approach without regard to the context of understanding and skill into which it's being flung is a mistake. Similarly the belief that playwrights are mere tape-recorders or transcribers of real-life dialogue. We go to theatre to be both reminded and transported. The successful realisation of an idea in theatre depends on the connective tissue of the narrative accommodating that stretch.

To come back finally to that thorny question 'What do you act when you act realism?', the answer has to lie in the first instance on what the playwright wants to draw attention to. In the second instance it depends on what the audience is ready to see. In between the two it depends on what actors are motivated to show. If you look closely at the pupil of an eye, you see a distorted reflection of what the eye itself is seeing. That may not be exactly what is in the mind's eye, but it's as close as we ever get to actually seeing it.

Index